W9-BZB-674

At Issue

| Cyberwarfare

Other Books in the At Issue Series

At Issue

31969025806281

| Cyberwarfare

Megan Manzano, Book Editor

GREENHAVEN
PUBLISHING

Published in 2018 by Greenhaven Publishing, LLC
353 3rd Avenue, Suite 255, New York, NY 10010

Articles in Greenhaven Publishing anthologies are often edited for length to meet page
requirements. In addition, original titles of these works are changed to clearly present
the main thesis and to explicitly indicate the author's opinion. Every effort is made to
ensure that Greenhaven Publishing accurately reflects the original intent of the authors.
Every effort has been made to trace the owners of the copyrighted material.

Cover image: LeoWolfert/Shutterstock.com

Library of Congress Cataloging-in-Publication Data

Names: Manzano, Megan, editor.
Title: Cyberwarfare / Megan Manzano, book editor.
Description: First Edition. | New York : Greenhaven Publishing, [2018] |
Series: At issue | Audience: Grade 9 to 12. | Includes bibliographical references and index.
Identifiers: LCCN 2017035963| ISBN 9781534502048
(library bound) | ISBN 9781534502109 (pbk.)
Subjects: LCSH: Cyberspace operations (Military science) | Cyberterrorism. | Computer crimes.
Classification: LCC U167.5.C92 C935 2017 | DDC 355.4/1--dc23
LC record available at https://lccn.loc.gov/2017035963

Manufactured in the United States of America

Website: http://greenhavenpublishing.com

Contents

Introduction

Cyberwarfare is frequently defined as an attack or attempt to damage the information networks or computer systems of another nation. These attacks can be conducted by an organization or country, often with the intent to gather information, cripple a network, or inflict harm. Cyberwarfare is a growing global threat as technology continues to advance and more businesses and individuals rely on the internet to thrive. Exacting punishment on those involved is a difficult task. As the term "cyberwarfare" is still loosely defined, it must be broken apart, examined, and put back together to fall under modern-day laws. There also aren't the same physical repercussions that would come from a land war or an outright assault.

One example is the 2007 attack on the Estonian government. Their web services were disabled, creating chaos for millions of Estonian citizens who were faced with spam messages when they tried to access media outlets and online banking services. Though Russian hackers were the believed culprit, it was never proven. This disturbance emphasized the need for cybersecurity and, in 2008, NATO established a cyber defense research center. They published the *Tallinn Manual 2.0*, which is a detailed account of how existing laws can apply to cyberwarfare. It encourages nations to work together and determine rules against such crimes so it will not affect civilians nor damage the military. Some experts criticize the manual for defining the effects of cyber violence as only physical—citing that unless tangible property needs replacement, it does not fall within the brackets of the law. This could apply to computer systems and their components, but the line is not a hundred percent clear.

The next major attack came in Iran in 2010, in the form of a computer worm known as Stuxnet. It operated in a series of steps: first by analyzing and targeting computer networks, second by replicating itself inside of these networks and, third, by infiltrating the computer system entirely. Once inside the system, the worm took control of the machinery and could have been spread to any neighboring machine. Unlike in Estonia, which had their government systems hacked, Stuxnet impacted an Iranian nuclear facility. The worm was first noticed when uranium centrifuges began to break. The cause wasn't immediately clear, but as technicians looked into the matter, they found the vicious and dangerous malware.

When examining governments and countries that rely heavily on the internet and connectivity for data storage and basic operations, it is not out of place to fear what a large-scale cyberattack could accomplish. The military, financial data, means of travel, communication, and power grids could all be shut down. There are some serious questions to be raised about what defenses countries can mount in this kind of scenario.

Concerns must also be raised for the everyday internet user. Between the reliance on technology and more companies moving towards a digital platform, scams exist everywhere. From spam-filled advertisements, to clickbait links, to a trojan-filled app downloaded on one's phone, there are countless opportunities for a hacker to steal personal information or monitor someone via a webcam. The more technology advances, the less privacy an individual has. Thousands of identities are stolen annually with the victim none the wiser.

The biggest challenge when it comes to cyberattacks is discerning proper response and punishment. One idea for combating cyberwarfare is to implement global governance, a transnational approach to developing solutions instead of one individual government. This comes with its own set of problems such as monitoring and enforcing the laws as well as mutual cooperation and what that would mean from a multitude of nations. It seems daunting, but having a coalition come together—as opposed to no cooperation at all—could only better protect the public, the global economy, and the internet.

Identifying the crime and the criminal who is doing the hacking is another hurdle in the battle against cyberwarfare. Taking hackers into custody can prove difficult, given the laws and jurisdiction of the countries in which they live. There is, too, the expansiveness of the internet and the Dark Web, which provides ample room to seek refuge—hackers often have ways of hiding their identity or losing themselves within the secret servers they tap into. Suddenly, the criminal gets further and further away from the source, blurring their identity and making accountability impossible.

To prevent cyberattacks, one must be both vigilant and educated. *At Issue: Cyberwarfare* explores the roots of cyberwarfare as well as the complexities and controversial ideas that come with combatting such an alarming and insidious threat to global security.

1

The Impact of Cybersecurity

Eric A. Fischer

Eric Fischer is the senior specialist in science and technology at the Congressional Research Service of the Library of Congress. He provides expert advice to the US Congress on various issues in science and technology policy, including cybersecurity, election reform, and the environment.

Cyberattacks have been on the rise in recent years, leading to a number of long- and short-term challenges, which are touched upon in the following piece. Information and communication technology (ICT) has had to update existing cybersecurity procedures and implement entirely new procedures in order to protect systems, but Fischer outlines how more action needs to be taken on a legislative and governmental level if global technology is to remain truly secure.

[...]

The Concept of Cybersecurity

Over the past several years, experts and policymakers have expressed increasing concerns about protecting ICT systems from *cyberattacks*—deliberate attempts by unauthorized persons to access ICT systems, usually with the goal of theft, disruption, damage, or other unlawful actions. Many experts expect the number and severity of cyberattacks to increase over the next several years[1].

"Cybersecurity Issues and Challenges: In Brief," by Eric A. Fischer, Federation of American Scientists, August 12, 2016.

The act of protecting ICT systems and their contents has come to be known as *cybersecurity*. A broad and arguably somewhat fuzzy concept, cybersecurity can be a useful term but tends to defy precise definition. It usually refers to one or more of three things:

- A set of activities and other measures intended to protect—from attack, disruption, or other threats—computers, computer networks, related hardware and devices software and the information they contain and communicate, including software and data, as well as other elements of cyberspace[2].
- The state or quality of being protected from such threats.
- The broad field of endeavor aimed at implementing and improving those activities and quality[3].

It is related to but not generally regarded as identical to the concept of *information security*, which is defined in federal law (44 U.S.C. §3552(b)(3)) as:

Protecting information and information systems from unauthorized access, use, disclosure, disruption, modification, or destruction in order to provide-

(A) integrity, which means guarding against improper information modification or destruction, and includes ensuring information nonrepudiation and authenticity;

(B) confidentiality, which means preserving authorized restrictions on access and disclosure, including means for protecting personal privacy and proprietary information; and

(C) availability, which means ensuring timely and reliable access to and use of information.

Cybersecurity is also sometimes conflated inappropriately in public discussion with other concepts such as privacy, information sharing, intelligence gathering, and surveillance. Privacy is associated with the ability of an individual person to control access by others to information about that person. Thus, good cybersecurity can help protect privacy in an electronic environment, but information that is shared to assist in cybersecurity efforts might sometimes contain personal information that at least some observers would regard as private. Cybersecurity can be a means of protecting against undesired surveillance of and gathering of intelligence from an information system. However, when aimed at potential sources of cyberattacks, such activities can also be useful to help effect cybersecurity. In addition, surveillance in the form of monitoring of information flow within a system can be an important component of cybersecurity[4].

Management of Cybersecurity Risks

The risks associated with any attack depend on three factors: *threats* (who is attacking), *vulnerabilities* (the weaknesses they are attacking), and *impacts* (what the attack does). The management of risk to information systems is considered fundamental to effective cybersecurity[5].

What Are the Threats?

People who actually or potentially perform cyberattacks are widely cited as falling into one or more of five categories: *criminals* intent on monetary gain from crimes such as theft or extortion; spies intent on stealing classified or proprietary information used by government or private entities; *nation-state warriors* who develop capabilities and undertake cyberattacks in support of a country's strategic objectives; *"hacktivists"* who perform cyberattacks for nonmonetary reasons; and *terrorists* who engage in cyberattacks as a form of non-state or state-sponsored warfare.

What Are the Vulnerabilities?

Cybersecurity is in many ways an arms race between attackers and defenders. ICT systems are very complex, and attackers are constantly probing for weaknesses, which can occur at many points. Defenders can often protect against weaknesses, but three are particularly challenging: inadvertent or intentional acts by *insiders* with access to a system; *supply chain* vulnerabilities, which can permit the insertion of malicious software or hardware during the acquisition process; and previously unknown, or *zero-day*, vulnerabilities with no established fix. Even for vulnerabilities where remedies are known, they may not be implemented in many cases because of budgetary or operational constraints.

What Are the Impacts?

A successful attack can compromise the confidentiality, integrity, and availability of an ICT system and the information it handles. *Cybertheft* or *cyberespionage* can result in exfiltration of financial, proprietary, or personal information from which the attacker can benefit, often without the knowledge of the victim. *Denial-of-service* attacks can slow or prevent legitimate users from accessing a system. Botnet malware can give an attacker command of a system for use in cyberattacks on other systems. Attacks on *industrial control systems* can result in the destruction or disruption of the equipment they control, such as generators, pumps, and centrifuges.

Most cyberattacks have limited impacts, but a successful attack on some components of critical infrastructure (CI)—most of which is held by the private sector—could have significant effects on national security, the economy, and the livelihood and safety of individual citizens. Thus, a rare successful attack with high impact can pose a larger risk than a common successful attack with low impact.

While it is widely recognized that cyberattacks can be costly to individuals and organizations, economic impacts can be difficult to measure, and estimates of those impacts vary widely. An often cited figure for annual cost to the global economy from cybercrime is $400 billion, with some observers arguing that costs are increasing substantially, especially with the continued expansion of ICT infrastructure through the Internet of Things and other new and emerging platforms[6]. The costs of cyberespionage can be even more difficult to quantify but are considered to be substantial[7].

Managing the risks from cyberattacks usually involves (1) removing the threat source (e.g., by closing down botnets or reducing incentives for cybercriminals); (2) addressing vulnerabilities by hardening ICT assets (e.g., by patching software and training employees); and (3) lessening impacts by mitigating damage and restoring functions (e.g., by having back-up resources available for continuity of operations in response to an attack). The optimal level of risk reduction will vary among sectors and organizations. For example, the level of cybersecurity that customers expect may be lower for a company in the entertainment sector than for a bank, a hospital, or a government agency.

Federal Role

The federal role in cybersecurity involves both securing federal systems and assisting in protecting nonfederal systems. Under current law, all federal agencies have cybersecurity responsibilities relating to their own systems, and many have sector-specific responsibilities for CI. More than 50 statutes address various aspects of cybersecurity.

In February 2015, the Obama Administration also established, via presidential memorandum, the Cyber Threat Intelligence Integration Center (CTIIC) under the Director of National Intelligence (DNI). Its purposes are to provide integrated analysis on cybersecurity threats and incidents affecting national interests across the federal government and to support relevant government entities, including the NCCIC and others at DOD and DOJ.

Federal Spending

Federal agencies spend a significant part of their annual IT funding on cybersecurity, which currently constitutes 16-17% (about one in every seven dollars) of agency IT budgets overall. However, DOD spending accounts for a large proportion of that expenditure, ranging from 22–30% of the DOD IT budget from FY2010 to FY2015. The median proportion for other agencies has been 6-7% during that period. That is roughly equivalent to spending patterns for businesses of 4–9% reported in a recent survey[8].

The FY2017 budget request includes over $19 billion altogether for cybersecurity. With a total requested IT investment of $81.6 billion, that would amount to a proportion of 23.3%, or about one in every four dollars, to be spent on cybersecurity. For more information on federal cybersecurity spending, see CRS Report R44404, *Perspectives on Federal Cybersecurity Spending*, by William L. Painter and Chris Jaikaran.

Legislative Proposals and Actions

Since at least the 111th Congress, many bills have been introduced that would address a range of cybersecurity issues:

- **Cybercrime Laws**—updating criminal statutes and law-enforcement authorities relating to cybersecurity.
- **Data-Breach Notification**—requiring notification to victims and other responses after data breaches involving personal or financial information of individuals.
- **FISMA Reform**—updating the law to reflect changes in ICT and the threat landscape.
- **Information Sharing**—easing access of the private sector to classified and unclassified threat information and removing barriers to sharing within the private sector and with the federal government.
- **Internet of Things**—addressing a range of cybersecurity issues arising from the proliferation of devices and objects (such as home appliances, automobiles, medical devices, factories, and infrastructure) connected to the internet.
- **Privately Held CI**—improving protection of private-sector CI from attacks with major impacts.
- **R&D**—updating agency authorizations and strategic planning requirements.
- **Workforce**—improving the size, skills, and preparation of the federal and private sector cybersecurity workforce.

[...]

Executive Branch Actions

Some notable actions have been taken by the Obama Administration during the 114th Congress. Some of the provisions in the enacted legislation provided statutory authority for programs or activities previously established through executive action. In addition to the

NCCIC (P.L. 113282), examples include the Scholarship for Service program and the NIST cybersecurity framework process (P.L. 113-274), as well as the EINSTEIN intrusion-protection program for federal agencies (P.L. 114-113). The Administration has also taken steps to implement enacted provisions.

Additional actions include the following:

- Executive Order 13691 set up mechanisms to promote the widespread use of information sharing and analysis organizations and the development of standards for their establishment and operation.
- Subsequent to significant data breaches, such as the 2015 exfiltration of records from the Office of Personnel Management (see CRS Report R44111, *Cyber Intrusion into U.S. Office of Personnel Management: In Brief*, coordinated by Kristin Finklea), and other concerns, the Administration announced a cybersecurity national action plan to implement strategies to enhance U.S. cybersecurity nationwide. Initiatives in the plan include a proposed revolving fund for modernizing federal IT (see H.R. 4897 and H.R. 5792) and the appointment of a federal chief information security officer, among other actions.
- Presidential Policy Directive 41 describes how the federal government will respond to cybersecurity incidents affecting government and private-sector entities, including principles, kinds of response, a framework of roles and responsibilities, and coordination.

Long-Term Challenges

The legislative and executive-branch actions discussed above are largely designed to address several well-established near-term needs in cybersecurity: preventing cyber-based disasters and espionage, reducing impacts of successful attacks, improving inter- and intrasector collaboration, clarifying federal agency roles and responsibilities, and fighting cybercrime. However, those needs exist in the context of more difficult long-term challenges relating to design, incentives, consensus, and environment (DICE):

Design: Experts often say that effective security needs to be an integral part of ICT design. Yet, developers have traditionally focused more on features than security, for economic reasons. Also, many future security needs cannot be predicted, posing a difficult challenge for designers.

Incentives: The structure of economic incentives for cybersecurity has been called distorted or even perverse. Cybercrime is regarded as cheap, profitable, and comparatively safe for the criminals. In contrast, cybersecurity can be expensive, is by its nature imperfect, and the economic returns on investments are often unsure.

Consensus: Cybersecurity means different things to different stakeholders, often with little common agreement on meaning, implementation, and risks. Substantial cultural impediments to consensus also exist, not only between sectors but within sectors and even within organizations. Traditional approaches to security may be insufficient in the hyperconnected environment of cyberspace, but consensus on alternatives has proven elusive.

Environment: Cyberspace has been called the fastest evolving technology space in human history, both in scale and properties. New and emerging properties and applications—especially social media, mobile computing, big data, cloud computing, and the Internet of Things—further complicate the evolving threat environment, but they can also pose potential opportunities for improving cybersecurity, for example through the economies of scale provided by cloud computing and big data analytics.

Legislation and executive actions in the 114th and future Congresses could have significant impacts on those challenges. For example, cybersecurity R&D may affect the design of ICT, cybercrime penalties may influence the structure of incentives, the NIST framework may facilitate achievement of a consensus on cybersecurity, and federal initiatives in cloud computing and other new components of cyberspace may help shape the evolution of cybersecurity.

Notes

1. See, for example, Lee Rainie, Janna Anderson, and Jennifer Connolly, *Cyber Attacks Likely to Increase* (Pew Research Internet Project, October 2014), http://www. pewInternet.org/2014/10/29/cyber-attacks-likely-to-increase/.

2. The term *cyberspace* usually refers to the worldwide collection of connected ICT components, the information that is stored in and flows through those components, and the ways that information is structured and processed.

3. For a more in-depth discussion of this concept, see CRS Report RL32777, Creating a National Framework for *Cybersecurity: An Analysis of Issues and Options*, by Eric A. Fischer.

4. See, for example, Department of Homeland Security, "Continuous Diagnostics and Mitigation (CDM)," June 24, 2014, http://www.dhs.gov/cdm.

5. See, for example, National Institute of Standards and Technology, *Managing Information Security Risk: Organization, Mission, and Information System View*, March 2011, http://csrc.nist.gov/publications/nistpubs/800-39/ SP800-39-final.pdf.

6. See, for example, Center for Strategic and International Studies, "Net Losses: Estimating the Global Cost of Cybercrime" (McAfee, June 2014), http://www.mcafee.com/us/resources/reports/rp-economic-impactcybercrime2.pdf?cid=BHP028; Cybersecurity Ventures, "Cybersecurity Market Report, Q2 2016," 2016, http://cybersecurityventures.com/cybersecurity-market-report/. For more information on the Internet of Things, see CRS Report R44227, *The Internet of Things: Frequently Asked Questions*, by Eric A. Fischer.

7. Office of the National Counterintelligence Executive, "Foreign Spies Stealing U.S. Economic Secrets in Cyberspace: Report to Congress on Foreign Economic Collection and Industrial Espionage, 2009-2011," October 2011, https://www.dni.gov/files/documents/Newsroom/Reports%20and%20Pubs/20111103_report_fecie.pdf.

8. Barbara Filkins, "IT Security Spending Trends" (SANS Institute, February 2016), https://www.sans.org/readingroom/whitepapers/analyst/security-spending-trends-36697. The results are from a survey of 169 organizations across several sectors that found median proportions of 4-6% for FY2014 and 7-9% for FY2016.

2

Cyberattacks: A New Threat

Marc Ginsberg

Former ambassador to Morocco Marc Ginsberg serves as a special adviser to the Department of Defense Special Operations Command and an adviser to the US Department of State on outreach initiatives to the Muslim world.

The threat of cyberattacks is growing around the world. Criminal hackers are finding ways to tap into security systems claimed to be under lock and key, creating a new kind of terrorism. Ambassador Ginsberg offers his unique perspective on the issue in this write-up from 2016, stressing that "Cybercrime is cyber terrorism." He asserts that countries and corporations have been "woefully reactive" and must craft stronger responses to cyberattacks and "new types of internet shields."

Between Pope Francis' extraordinary U.S. visit and Mr. Putin's double-down to save Syria's Assad, Chinese President Xi Jinping's state visit came close to becoming an "*" in the annals of major comings and goings. On *60 Minutes* last evening President Obama devoted nary a word to China - not its South China Sea "sandperialism" nor its cyberespionage. President Xi is not too far off in anti-U.S. attitudes than his comrade Vladimir Putin. But unlike Russia, China has repeatedly attacked our homeland breaching our internet firewalls to a degree that is downright disastrous to our national security.

"Cyber Warfare and the New Digital Arms Race," by Amb. Marc Ginsberg, Huffington Post, October 12, 2016. Reprinted by Permission.

The worst kept secret in Washington is that China "cyberhacked" 5.6 million fingerprints and personnel files of federal employee files from the Office of Personnel Management. We're not talking run-of-the-mill civil servants. OPM has in its personnel files Americans who hold top secret clearances. This high crime and misdemeanor establishes the condition for decades of accelerated official Chinese blackmail and devious conduct against Americans most engaged in protecting the homeland against Chinese espionage.

According to recent testimony by James Lewis, Director of Strategic Technologies Programs at the Center for Strategic and International Studies before the House Committee on Foreign Affairs on September 30, 2015, Chinese cybercriminals—private and public—are responsible for more than half of all economic espionage against the U.S.—more than all the countries of the world put together (mind you, it's no secret that the U.S. engages in similar attacks, as well). Russians prefer targeting U.S. financial institutions and drilling into State Department and political data - including President Obama's daily schedule which the Russians hacked right out of the White House's computer network sent across an unclassified computer network.

Rather than slap on economic sanctions as would be fitting, President Obama's kittenish National Security staff preferred holding the heavy artillery. Instead, China's audacious cyberespionage campaign did yield a tentative/tentative concession from Xi during his visit. China and the U.S. agreed not to direct or support cyberattacks that breach corporate firewalls for economic benefit. In plain English, Xi committed (as did the U.S.) to stop hacking into the corporate patents and trade secrets of U.S. companies. Who is going to bet the mortgage that Beijing will honor its pledge? I'd like to see NSC Adviser Susan Rice back this up with her mortgage—fat chance—even though she touted this as a significant accomplishment from the Xi-Obama Summit.

On October 19 at the Union League Club in New York the C3 Summit—a major conference on cybersecurity and the palliative response of retooled "smart cities"—will occur to address the threat of cyberthreats to our urban landscape. The conference will geographically focus on the tinderbox of the Middle East and how cyber risk mitigation can play a critical role pacifying the threat that cyberespionage and terror-laced social media by ISIS—and a prescriptive internet landscape that could emerge to jump-start new investment in the region. The conference will also address what major U.S. technologies are in development to thwart cyberwarfare. I am looking forward to vacuuming up the data from the conference to explore what more preemptive risk mitigation can be undertaken to protect American companies and those entities fighting terrorism to protect our national security.

For attribution I have no pecuniary gain, role, or responsibility for the C3Summit. It just happens to be loaded up with some interesting speakers and topics relating to this article.

The growing threat of destructive cyberattacks is evident from every corner of the globe. Whether it be from Iran, Cuba, North Korea, and Eastern European criminals hacking into your checking accounts, let alone Target or name a dozen other high-profile consumer companies who thought they had credit card info under computer lock and key. Several years ago, the Kremlin launched a debilitating cyberattack against Estonia . . . crippling its entire internet network, government computers, and financial institutions. Just a taste of things to come. According to today's *Wall Street Journal*, at least 29 countries have formal military or intelligence units dedicated to offensive hacking efforts. The so-called digital battlefield includes a range of funny sounding, but ominously deadly names and acronyms that are invented and reinvented in a constant struggle to breach the best of computer network defenses.

Cybercrime is cyber terrorism. Just think what the Pentagon has to contend with. Hackers only have to succeed once in their attack, while defenders have to maintain a 24/7 vigilance. The rate of serious attacks that have destroyed networks, stolen classified info, infiltrated personal data, or robbed sizable sums from financial institutions from 2009 to 2014 is 66 percent. The

Department of Homeland Security recently awarded a massive cybersecurity contract to Raytheon to the tune of $1 billion to create an "impenetrable" cyber fire wall against the onslaught of attacks. Raytheon also is in the vanguard of attracting the best counter-hacker talent. It is a finalist in a $2 million Grand Cyber Challenge—a competition initiated by the Defense Department's cyber research arm.

What Raytheon and other IT companies are undertaking takes on even greater importance in the age of "the Internet of Things." When your smartphone becomes the remote control for your bank account, to your prescription drug ordering or from your home security switch to your car ignition—the grim hacker possibilities grow exponentially.

Countries, like corporations, have been woefully reactive to cybercrimes. IT professionals barely can stay one step ahead of devious cybercriminals, many of who are on the payroll of our adversaries. Creating malicious code in the guise of "phishing" or malware has reached such epidemic proportions that many of my friends' email addresses and their address books have been usurped with innocent-looking links, which are anything but. How many of you have received emails from friends barely avoiding clicking on a link that may innocuously say something like "take a look at our latest pix from vacation."

Cyberweaponry requires cyberdeterrence and new types of internet shields. Major U.S. corporations spend millions repairing damage from cyber infiltration, but devote hardly any resources to assessing potential risk sources and pre-emptive mitigation. Cybersleuthing represents a new 21st-century opportunity for risk assessment firms which can provide crucial intelligence and help map out for unsuspecting corporations likely sources of criminal cyber mischief. The urgent need for cybersecurity firms to retool themselves in order to implement deterrence and pre-emptive cyberattack warning salvos is growing by the day.

3

Consequences of a Cyberattack

Lin Yang Kang

Yang Kang is a naval officer from the Republic of Singapore and, at the time of publication, a student at the Nanyang Technological University (NTU) in Singapore studying Electrical and Electronics Engineering.

Real-world examples of cyberattacks demonstrate how quickly a network system can be crippled. As the following piece details, these attacks can come quickly and without warning, leaving the victims flailing for options to retaliate without concrete proof or avenues for recovering data. According to Kang, more global defenses need to be in place and "the rules of cyber warfare need to be clarified and be abided by the international community to safeguard civilians."

The Internet has grown phenomenally since the 1990s and currently has about 3.5 billion users who make up 47 percent of the world population.[1] Out of the 201 countries surveyed, 38 percent have a penetration rate of at least 80 percent of its population.[2] The ubiquity and reliance on cyberspace to improve the efficiency and capability of government, military, and civilian sectors lead to the Internet of Things (IOT) for day-to-day operations and in this pervasiveness of the use of Internet lies the potential for devastating cyber-attacks.

"The Threat, Defense, and Control of Cyber Warfare," by Lin Yang Kang, Center for International Maritime Security, April 17, 2017. Reprinted by Permission.

This paper seeks to discuss the crippling effects and dangers of cyber-attacks and outline the defensive responses against and control of cyber warfare.

The lethality, and hence appeal of cyber warfare, lies in its asymmetric[3] and stealthy nature. Little resource, such as teams of experienced hackers, is required to render a disproportional amount of devastating damage to the core and day-to-day operations of both the government as well as the military. Unlike conventional warfare where a military build-up and transportation of resources are tell-tale signs of preparation, cyber-attacks can be conducted without warning. In this regard, it is akin to covert operations, such as the use of Special Forces or submarines, with added advantage of not exposing soldiers to the risk of harm. Coupled with the inherent difficulty in pinpointing attribution,[4] subjects of a cyber-attack are left with the choice of either doing nothing except to try to recover or to retaliate against the suspected attacker without concrete proof and lose moral high ground, neither of which is optimal.

An example of a well-coordinated attack demonstrating the covert nature of cyber warfare occurred in 2007 when the Estonian government and government-related web-services were disabled.[5] Though no physical damage was inflicted, it created widespread disruption for Estonian citizens. While Russia was the suspected perpetrator, it was never proven or acknowledged. In 2010, it was discovered that Iranian nuclear centrifuges that are responsible for enriching uranium gas had been infected and crippled by a malware, codenamed "Stuxnet."[6] This successful insertion of this malware effectively set the Iranian nuclear program back for a few years and demonstrated an effective and non-attributable way[7] to pressurize if not exert will without the use of military might as it achieved what the United Nations Security Council (UNSC) had hitherto failed to do, i.e., curtail the development of nuclear weapons by Iran.

The above examples illustrate the potential damage of small-scale and limited cyber-attacks. Extrapolating from these examples, it is conceivable that the damage from a successful large-scale cyber-attack on a well-connected country that relies heavily on IOT can range from disruption of essential services, crippling confusion and even operational paralysis of both government and the military. For the government, a cyber-attack across every essential means and aspects of daily living including but not limited to destruction of financial data, records and transactions, forms of travel, communication means, and national power grid create chaos and confusion resulting in psychological shock that will in turn sap the will and resilience of the citizens. For the military, the irony is that the more modern and advanced a military is with its concomitant reliance on technology and network centric warfare, the more vulnerable it is to a potential cyber Pearl Harbor attack that will render its technological superiority over its adversary impotent. Given the symbiotic relation between the government and the military, a successful simultaneous cyber-attack on both government and the military can achieve Sun Tze's axiom that the supreme art of war is to subdue the enemy without fighting.

Given its unique nature and unmatched demonstrated potential for lethality, it is understandable the attractiveness of cyber warfare as an instrument of choice for all players, both state and non-state actors and even individuals. As with all other forms of warfare, the need for defense against should be proportional to the threat. It is a game of cat and mouse,[8] where hackers seek to find security vulnerabilities while defenders attempt to patch them up as soon as they are exploited and redirect the attackers to digital traps, preventing them from obtaining crucial information or cause damages. Specialized cyber warfare military branches have been formed in many countries, and extensive cyber defensive measures and contingency plans are being developed by government, military, and civil sectors of states. Through inter-cooperation, potential attacks could be resolved in the shortest time possible and minimize disruption, while preventing future attacks. As the world begins to witness the increasing use of cyber warfare as a weapon, cyber-attacks may not be as easy to conduct as before as states that understand the lethality of such attacks seek to safeguard their nation.[9]

Beyond defense at the national level, there is a lack of well-defined norms on the rules of cyber warfare as the international law community is still interpreting how current law of war can apply to cyber warfare. Recently, *Tallinn Manual 2.0* was published by NATO's Cooperative Cyber Defence Centre of Excellence (CCDOE) and is to date the most detailed study of how existing international laws can govern cyber operations.[10] However, it currently serves as a reference and is non-binding. It is crucial for nations to iron out the rules for cyber warfare together and abide by it, ensuring that it will not affect the lives of civilians and minimize potential damages to non-military installations by cyber-attacks and cyber warfare.

Cyber warfare is a real and growing threat which has the potential to create disruption that the world has yet to witness. As nations become even more reliant on cyberspace as it ventures into automation and smart cities, they need to invest adequately in cyber defense and ensure that this new frontier is well-guarded. Apart from dealing with it domestically, on an international level, rules of cyber warfare need to be clarified and be abided by the international community to safeguard civilians. Cyber warfare may be threatening, but if the international community abides by clarified rules of cyber warfare and has sufficient cyber defensive measures established, the potential devastation caused by cyber-attacks could be minimized.

Bibliography

Barker, Colin. "Hackers and defenders continue cybersecurity game of cat and mouse." ZDNet. February 04, 2016. Accessed March 28, 2017. http://www.zdnet.com/article/hackers-and-defenders-continue-cyber-security-game-of-cat-and-mouse.

Davis, Joshua. "Hackers Take Down the Most Wired Country in Europe." *Wired*. August 21, 2007. Accessed March 21, 2017. https://www.wired.com/2007/08/ff-estonia.

Geers, Kenneth. *Strategic cyber security*. Tallinn: NATO Cooperative Cyber Defence Centre of Excellence, 2011.

"Cyber Warfare Integral Part of Modern Politics, New Analysis Reaffirms." NATO Cooperative Cyber Defence Centre of Excellence. December 01, 2015. Accessed March 15, 2017. https://ccdcoe.org/cyber-warfare-integral-part-modern-politics-new-analysis-reaffirms.html.

"Global Cybersecurity Index & Cyberwellness Profiles Report." April 2015. Accessed March 23, 2017. https://www.itu.int/dms_pub/itu-d/opb/str/D-STR-SECU-2015-PDF-E.pdf.

"NATO presents the Tallinn Manual 2.0 on International Law Applicable to cyberspace." Security Affairs. February 05, 2017. Accessed March 25, 2017. http://securityaffairs.co/wordpress/56004/cyber-warfare-2/nato-tallinn-manual-2-0.html.

"Internet Users." Number of Internet Users (2016) – Internet Live Stats. Accessed March 20, 2017. http://www.internetlivestats.com/internet-users.

"Internet Users by Country (2016)." Internet Users by Country (2016) – Internet Live Stats. Accessed March 20, 2017. http://www.internetlivestats.com/internet-users-by-country.

"The Asymmetric Nature of Cyber Warfare." USNI News. February 05, 2013. Accessed March 20, 2017. https://news.usni.org/2012/10/14/asymmetric-nature-cyber-warfare.

"The Attribution Problem in Cyber Attacks." InfoSec Resources. July 19, 2013. Accessed March 25, 2017. http://resources.infosecinstitute.com/attribution-problem-in-cyber-attacks/#gref.

Zetter, Kim. "An Unprecedented Look at Stuxnet, the World's First Digital Weapon." *Wired.* November 03, 2014. Accessed March 21, 2017. https://www.wired.com/2014/11/countdown-to-zero-day-stuxnet.

Notes

1. "Internet Users." Number of Internet Users (2016) – Internet Live Stats. Accessed March 20, 2017. http://www.internetlivestats.com/internet-users.

2. "Internet Users by Country (2016)." Internet Users by Country (2016) – Internet Live Stats. Accessed March 20, 2017. http://www.internetlivestats.com/internet-users-by-country.

3. "The Asymmetric Nature of Cyber Warfare." USNI News. February 05, 2013. Accessed March 20, 2017. https://news.usni.org/2012/10/14/asymmetric-nature-cyber-warfare.

4. "The Attribution Problem in Cyber Attacks." InfoSec Resources. July 19, 2013. Accessed March 25, 2017. http://resources.infosecinstitute.com/attribution-problem-in-cyber-attacks/#gref.

5. Davis, Joshua. "Hackers Take Down the Most Wired Country in Europe." *Wired.* August 21, 2007. Accessed March 21, 2017. https://www.wired.com/2007/08/ff-estonia.

6. Zetter, Kim. "An Unprecedented Look at Stuxnet, the World's First Digital Weapon." *Wired.* November 03, 2014. Accessed March 21, 2017. https://www.wired.com/2014/11/countdown-to-zero-day-stuxnet.

7. The United States and Israel were allegedly responsible for this cyber attacked but as with the Estonian example, it was never proven or acknowledged.

8. Barker, Colin. "Hackers and defenders continue cybersecurity game of cat and mouse." ZDNet. February 04, 2016. Accessed March 28, 2017. http://www.zdnet.com/article/hackers-and-defenders-continue-cyber-security-game-of-cat-and-mouse.

9. "Global Cybersecurity Index & Cyberwellness Profiles Report." April 2015. Accessed March 23, 2017. https://www.itu.int/dms_pub/itu-d/opb/str/D-STR-SECU-2015-PDF-E.pdf.

10. "NATO presents the Tallinn Manual 2.0 on International Law Applicable to cyberspace." Security Affairs. February 05, 2017. Accessed March 25, 2017. http://securityaffairs.co/wordpress/56004/cyber-warfare-2/nato-tallinn-manual-2-0.html.

4

What Cybercrime Means for Privacy

Merlin Oommen

India-based writer Merlin Oommen has a M.A in Media Governance from New Delhi's Jamia Millia Islamia. Currently employed at a media research company which helps both Indian and transnational corporations achieve their communication goals, she has also worked as an intern at the Centre for Internet and Society.

During the 1960s and 1970s, cybercrime meant physically damaging a system. Today, it often involves collecting all kinds of personal data using sophisticated software—meaning true privacy cannot exist on the internet. In the following article from 2011, Merlin Oommen takes a look at cybersecurity in India and around the globe and asks a very important question: If "secure" websites can't protect themselves from hackers, how can they protect the private information of users who access their services?

Introduction

India is a growing area in the field of active Internet usage with 71 million Internet users.[1] "Cyberspace is shorthand for the Web of consumer electronics; computers and communication networks that interconnect the World".[2] The recent incidents of hacking into various popular websites of Yahoo!, CNN, Sony, the CBI and the Indian Army raise the very pertinent issue of online data privacy. This blog will examine the growing instances of hacking websites and its impact on data privacy.

Cybercrime

"Cybercrime is a criminal offence on the Web, a criminal offence regarding the Internet, a violation of law on the Internet, an illegality committed with regard to the Internet, breach of law on the Internet, computer crime, contravention through the Web, corruption regarding Internet, disrupting operations through malevolent programs on the Internet, electric crime, sale of contraband on the Internet, stalking victims on the Internet and theft of identity on the Internet."[3]

The computer age gave rise to a new field of crime namely "cybercrime" or "computer crime". During the 1960s and 1970s cybercrime involved physical damage to the consumer system. Gradually computers were attacked using more sophisticated modus operandi where individuals would hack into the operating system to gain access to consumer files. The 1970s—through to the present—saw cybercrimes taking different trajectories like impersonation, credit card frauds, identity theft, and virus attacks, etc.[4]

The IT Act 2000 was enacted by the government to punish such acts of cybercrime. The Act was amended in the year 2008[5].

Cybercrime—An Overview: India

The IT Act 2000 was enacted by the government in 2000 to punish acts of cybercrime. The Act was amended in the year 2008[5]. According to the National Crime Records Bureau, cyber crime is on the rise. The Bureau reported that 420 cases were reported under the IT Act in the year 2009 alone, which was a 45.8 per cent increase from the year 2008. [6] The NCRB data on cyber crime also provides a useful insight as to the growing awareness of the IT Act. The data clearly shows an increase in the number of cases reported from the years 2005 to 2009.[7] Hacking and obscene [8] publication/transmission are the highest reported crimes with the highest rate of conviction under the IT Act 2008.

Cyberattack: No One Is Safe!!

In February 2000 the many "busy" Internet websites were jammed shut by hackers causing a national upheaval in the USA with the then President Clinton calling in a high-level meeting with experts from around the world. Websites like Yahoo.com were forced to shut down for three hours after they were "smurfed" by hackers.[9] Many other websites like Amazon.com and CNN.com were also attacked by the same hackers. Hacking such popular websites within a span of few hours was unprecedented which left many, including the FBI, clueless. By far these are the most serious cyberattacks in the history of Internet. The attacks not only shut down important sites, but also highlighted a very disturbing growing trend. If such popular websites were shut down by unknown perpetrators then how in the world will these and similar sites be able to protect scores of personal data and credit card information of the customers they pledge to serve?

More recently cybervandals attacked the US Senate website on the 14 June 2011, causing a huge security scare.[10] This instance again brings us to the pertinent question of the safety of our personal data held by these websites. If the personal data of the US Senators can be breached by somebody, then certainly we as consumers should be very wary of the cyberspace and its ability to protect our data.

Closer to Home

On June 8, a group claiming to be "anonymous" hacked into the government's National Information Centre to protest against the anti-graft agitation.[11] The same group was accused of hacking into the Indian Army's website although no report of data theft was claimed by the government. Last year in December a Pakistani hacker group named Predators PK hacked into various websites including the website of the CBI.[12]

Cybercrime: Its Implications to Privacy

Internet security has become an important issue. Recent cyberattacks on various important websites has placed many consumers at risk and vulnerable to cybercriminals. The hacking attack on the Sony website on April 16 and 17 led to the theft of 26.4 million SOE (Sony Online Enterprise) Accounts. The criminals even hacked into a 2007 database which held credit and debit card information of 23,400 customers.[13]

Attacks such as these demonstrate the vulnerability of websites, and the possibility of serious harm to a countries economy and security. Furthermore, consumers' personal data can be used by hackers to extort and blackmail individuals.

The Internet has become a huge stakeholder in facilitating trade and e-commerce, subsequently cyberspace has become a large network of communication and commerce. We carry out a number of tasks on the Internet—from e-shopping and e-ticketing to e-banking. Though the recent attacks on the CBI website, and the Indian Army website did catch some attention from the media, and the government did make some noise about it, the issue slowly faded away. The government cannot seem to protect its own websites which houses sensitive details of national security, but seems confident about putting personal data and biometrics of a billion plus population under the AADHAR scheme [14] onto a web server which can be hacked anytime by almost anybody with a personal computer in China or Pakistan.[15]

Privacy: No More?

Data generated in cyberspace are a fingerprint of an individual which is detailed, processed, and made permanent.[16] The cyberspace generates a blue print of our whole personality as we navigate through a health site, pay our bills, or shop for books at Amazon .com. The data collected by surfing through all these domains creates a fitting profile of who we are. [17] When hackers and cyber vandals steal this very information, it becomes a gross violation of our privacy.

Conclusion

Privacy does not exist in cyberspace. The various websites that offer varied services to its consumers fail to protect their personal data time and again. The Sony website including its play station and music website was hacked at least three times this year. Scores of personal data was stolen and the consumers were kept in dark regarding the breach for almost a week. Speaking as a consumer, if a large corporate company like Sony cannot protect its website from being hacked into, it is hard to imagine other websites protecting itself from attacks.

The rise of the Internet has brought with it a new dimension of crime. The IT Act 2000 has brought some reprieve to the aggrieved according to the NCRB. Despite this, the IT Act clearly will not completely deter criminals from hacking into websites, as was demonstrated in the NCRB report. The cybercriminals of the February 2000 cyberattacks have yet to be apprehended and the attacks on various websites have been increasing every year.

Despite progress being made on enacting cyberlaws and implementing them, cyber rime is still not nipped in the bud. Governments can do precious little to stop it and only hope that a cybercriminal can be traced back and be punished. Hence, Internet users need to more careful of the sites they visit; know the privacy policy of these websites to protect their personal data as much as possible.

Notes

1. According to an annual survey conducted by IMRB and Internet and Mobile Association of India for the year 2009 – 2010.

2. http://www.jstor.org/stable/pdfplus/1229286.pdf?acceptTC=true

3. http://legal-dictionary.thefreedictionary.com/cybercrime

4. http://www.mekabay.com/overviews/history.pdf

5. http://www.cyberlaws.net/itamendments/index1.htm

6. http://ncrb.nic.in/CII%202009/cii-2009/Chapter%2018.pdf

7. http://ncrb.nic.in/CII%202009/cii-2009/Chapter%2018.pdf

8. http://ncrb.nic.in/CII%202009/cii-2009/Chapter%2018.pdf

9. http://www.pbs.org/newshour/extra/features/jan-june00/hackers_2-17.html

10. http://in.reuters.com/article/2011/06/14/idININdia-57677720110614

11. http://www.thinkdigit.com/General/Anonymous-hacks-Indian-govt-website-to
    -support_6933.html

12. http://www.deccanherald.com/content/117901/pakistan-hackers-wage-cyber-war.html

13. http://mashable.com/2011/05/03/sony-another-hacker-attack/

14. http://uidai.gov.in/

15. http://www.securitywatchindia.org.in/selected_Article_Cyber_warfare.aspx

16. http://www.jstor.org/stable/pdfplus/1229286.pdf?acceptTC=true

17. http://www.jstor.org/stable/pdfplus/1229286.pdf?acceptTC=true

5

Smart Devices Lure in Hackers

Elad Ben-Meir

Elad Ben-Meir is the VP of marketing at CyberInt. Ben-Muir, who was educated at the Academic College of Tel-Aviv-Yaffo in Israel, also serves as a mentor at The Junction, a start-up accelerator and part of the Genesis Partners VC.

The Internet of Things (IoT), consisting of products such as smartphones or webcams, influences how hackers are able to access personal data and threaten a secure future. Threats that didn't exist years ago have become a reality, and as Elad Ben-Meir explains below, everything from smart fridges to commercial aircrafts face risks from cybercriminals. Though it's not yet a cause for widespread alarm, he warns that "Cyber attacks against critical infrastructures are not only referred to as 'nightmare scenarios,' they're also considered a matter of 'when, and not if.'"

IoT is a term coined by John Chambers, Cisco's CEO, which has become synonymous with a variety of products and devices like smartwatches, smart home and smart metering devices, augmented reality devices, and the likes. There are currently 16.3 billion IoT connected devices which are said to exist globally, and by 2020, the number will spike to 28.1 billion.

How does this affect our cyberthreat landscape? And by what means? What can past examples of IoT-caused threats teach us

"What Lures Cyber Criminals Towards the Internet of Things?" by Elad Ben-Meir, CyberInt, August 25, 2016. Reprinted by Permission.

for the future, so that we can begin to understand the hacker's mindset in planning these attacks?

The IoT Revolution

Bruce Schneier calls the IoT revolution that we're witnessing a "world-sized robot," which society is collectively building, without even realizing it's doing so.

Schneier elaborates:

> "With the advent of the Internet of Things and cyber-physical systems in general, we've given the internet hands and feet: the ability to directly affect the physical world. What used to be attacks against data and information have become attacks against flesh, steel, and concrete."

We've put together a few examples to try and understand the extent to which the IoT revolution poses a risk to society.

1. Augmented Reality → Remote Access Trojans

In mobile gaming, for example, augmented reality games are all the rage, such as the famed Pokémon Go which is now considered "the most popular augmented reality game yet created."

But as many know from past experience, **augmented reality is often an open invitation for cyberthreats.**

Remote Access

From the hacker's perspective, unofficial app stores are a sound attack vector for hackers to **gain full control over a victim's phone**. All they need to do, says Graham Cluley, is sneak their infected (unofficial) version of the app into the Google Play Store, which, as Cluley reminds us, "doesn't have a spotless record when it comes to keeping malware out."

This is the case with Pokémon Go, whose scam "wannabe" app versions allow APKs that include remote access tools such as DroidJack (also known as SandroRAT) into the Google Play Store.

DroidJack is a malware that specifically targets Android users and once it's installed, can access everything on the device.

Once the hacker gets this far on a victim's Android phone, all of the user's data can be accessed: email, contacts, photos, videos, text messages, or even the user's device camera or microphone.

This task becomes even simpler when unofficial marketplaces for apps are used. We've been witnessing a lot of cases where this happens, especially when there's a geographical restriction on the usage of certain apps (like Pokemon Go).

User Data → Company Data

Keep in mind that because the Pokémon Go app (along with many other apps out there) access the phone's GPS, clock and camera along other data, it can also **access Google's location data.**

By virtue of its use-case, Pokémon Go is "an app that is designed, from scratch, to track its users' whereabouts and behavior."

But the risks aren't posed against the end users (players) alone; the game **endangers companies all the same, even if they have no involvement or interest in the game itself.**

It goes without saying that if the phone also contains (or even accesses) sensitive corporate information at some stage, and not on a frequent/recurring basis, **then the company lies at risk as well.**

2. Critical Infrastructures → Data Exfiltration And Theft

Cyberattacks against critical infrastructures are not only referred to as "nightmare scenarios," they're also considered a matter of "when, and not if."

Because critical infrastructures all depend on giant IT networks, that incorporate IoT devices, they require cyberdefenses that are just as powerful as they are large.

Just how big of an issue are we talking about? In 2015, the U.S Department of Homeland Security's Industrial Control Systems Cybersecurity Emergency Response Team (ICS-CERT) **responded to 295 cyberincidents** (a 20% increase from the previous year).

Operation Dust Storm

A particularly notorious cyberattack on critical infrastructures was Operation Dust Storm, a multi-year, multi-attack campaign against companies in Japan, South Korea, the U.S. and Europe. Different targets included: electric utilities, oil and gas, finance, transportation and construction.

The attack began in 2010 (and continues to this day), when the criminal group began a series of attacks tactics to breach corporate networks and Android-based mobile devices. The attack methods included: spear phishing, waterholes, unique backdoors, zero-day variants, to name a few.

A true case study for a particularly gruesome example of the Cyber Kill Chain in its fullest sense, Operation Dust Storm teaches us the dire need to prevent materializing threats from their earliest stages of reconnaissance, to avoid being in a case of "too little too late."

3. Smart Devices (I.e. Smart Fridge) → Man-In-The-Middle Attacks

An SSL vulnerability was recently found on a line of Samsung smart fridges, in a penetration test that was part of an IoT hacking challenge, at the recent DefCon "IoT Village" hacking conference.

Because the inter-connected fridge is programmed to download Gmail Calendar information to an on-screen display, it threatens the Google credentials of the smart fridge users.

(Background: the smart fridge runs Google calendar so that its users can manage and view events from the fridge screen).

For this particular smart device (Samsung's RF28HMELBSR smart fridge), the weakness lies in its failure to validate SSL certificates—enabling man-in-the-middle attacks between the fridge and Google's servers.

Because the Gmail calendars on the smart fridge are downloaded from Google's server, it **becomes a lucrative attack vector for attackers to gain user credentials**.

During this specific series of penetration tests, other vulnerabilities were found as well: firmware attacks (a fake firmware update), TCP services and certificate challenges (found in the smart fridge's mobile app code).

4. Webcams → Remote Access Trojans

Be it the small cameras we have on our laptop screens, as in Zuckerberg's case above or baby monitoring cameras getting hacked into (scary!), webcams are vulnerable to remote access hacks. These are often appealing to cyber criminals, as they can be an easy way to steal sensitive corporate data or even worse, spy on our kids.

Once threat actors manage to install a malware on a computer, they can turn on that computer's camera and record or take a screenshot of what's going on.

Well-known public figures, such as Mark Zuckerberg, have each raised cyber awareness around the security threat behind webcams. In Zuckerberg's case, he did so inadvertently—when posing for a picture that was taken in front of his desk, and **his taped-over webcam and microphone appear** (by coincidence) in the background. From there, further inquiries were made…

Unlike hacks that stem from geo-location data, this malware can also exist on URL links, and as soon as a user clicks on one, his computer is open to vulnerabilities galore.

In addition to spying on users, hackers can send malicious emails on behalf of the hacked computer owner, or **launch a massive RAT attack to harm other computers** on his behalf, too.

Most recently, a webcam hack sob story was suffered by none other than Russia's Vladimir Putin, as part of the ongoing hacker blame game that's being exchanged between Russia and the DNC as part of the U.S presidential election campaign.

5. Commercial Aircraft → DDoS And Botnets

The aviation industry is a well-known destination for cybercriminals, or in other words, "a privileged target for hackers that are interested in the intellectual property of many companies in the sector."

But the reach of cyberattacks on airplanes are unprecedented; last year, a hacker hacked into the in-flight entertainment system on a United Airlines' aircraft, (and was able to do so 20 times during one flight), and overwrite the code on the plane's "Thrust Management Computer" while it was in the air, allowing him to monitor traffic from the cockpit system. Finally, he **issued a climb command and made the plane briefly change course**—"and caused one of the airplane engines to climb resulting in a lateral or sideways movement of the plane during one of these flights."

In other instances, hackers can flood flight management systems and control systems with a network of botnets, and cause the platform to crash.

At the end of the day, I don't truly think that this is a dooms day scenario where all the IoT devices will gang up and get rid of us humans. However, the IoT revolution does certainly expose us to additional (substantial) risk we were not accustomed to several years ago. We should be aware of these risks and manage them accordingly.

6

Is There Self-Defense Against Cyberattacks?

Jean-Marie Guéhenno

Former French diplomat Jean-Marie Guéhenno served as the United Nations' under secretary-general for peacekeeping operations between 2000 and 2008 and was appointed deputy joint special envoy for Syria by the United Nations and the Arab League in 2012. He now serves as president and CEO of the International Crisis Group.

The definition of war has become murkier as countries seem to engage in conflicts with no beginning or end. With the introduction of cyberwarfare, new challenges arise in defining what a self-defense strategy is and if it's even possible. Guéhenno notes that "power today is diffuse and it is shifting—mostly eastwards and southwards—in a manner that may prove as destabilizing as were the power shifts that came before the eruption of World War I."

Can we learn from past wars to prevent future ones? Or is the past a treacherous guide? What features dominate today's international peace and security landscape and how do they compare with those of a century ago? I will highlight three: a sense, perhaps misguided, that major instability in the West is unimaginable; a transformation in the nature of warfare; and a radically changed geostrategic context.

First, many in the West cannot imagine war in their own countries, partly because of the long stretch of peace we have

"The Transformation of War and Peace," by Jean-Marie Guéhenno, International Crisis Group, September 21, 2016. Reprinted by Permission.

enjoyed. European powers, for example, have not fought each other for 72 years—a period outstripping even the 44 years of peace preceding the First World War. This partly explains the trauma of terrorist attacks on Western public opinion. They do not inflict anything like the full pain of war, but their immediacy brings the conflicts of faraway places uncomfortably close to home.

The seeming remoteness of wars abroad, mirroring to some degree the colonial wars of the pre-1914 period, is further widened by the professionalization of the armies of the West today. This helps explain why Western politicians slip so easily into the language of war. Without conscription, war in fact directly impacts only very small segments of their societies.

Second, the nature of war has changed, with few parallels to wars of the previous century. Most wars are now civil wars, within states rather than between them, even if many of these same conflicts draw in outside powers. Non-state actors are among the main protagonists. Regional and even global powers influence or support—but rarely fully control—those fighting on the ground. The reality of this new type of war is painfully evident, for example, in Syria. Furthermore, some armed groups espouse radical and intolerant ideologies or transnational goals that are hard to accommodate in political settlements.

A definite separation between war and peace no longer exists. Many crises have no clear beginnings and no definitive ends. The world's most fragile countries are caught in cycles of instability, in which outbreaks of major fighting are interspersed with low-intensity violence and lawlessness. The U.S. itself has been fighting an open-ended war against al-Qaeda and its affiliates since 2001.

Today, only rarely is war ever "declared." The United Nations Charter, forged in the aftermath of World War II, limits the use of force—without a formal Security Council authorization—to self-defense. Self-defense is clear enough when troops cross a border. But what does "self-defense" mean when it comes to covert operations, unclaimed cyberattacks, "hybrid warfare," or a terrorist strike launched from a failed state?

Last, these changes are occurring in a geostrategic environment that has changed dramatically, even within the past decade. A century ago, Europe was the epicenter of the world and it was the main theater of war. Today, a more diverse group of powers have emerged, each of which is building their own military capacities and pursuing their own rivalries. The regional confrontation between Iran and Saudi Arabia. Tensions between China, Japan, and other Asian powers over maritime areas. The potentially explosive Pakistan-India rivalry. Geopolitical jockeying in Africa. These are all are cases in point.

Nor is the world ordered by a single geostrategic confrontation, as it was during the Cold War. The U.S., with its economic and military muscle and web of alliances, remains preeminent, yet the overall picture is more complex. In some ways, the trends should move us toward greater peace, as exchanges of trade, capital, and people connect countries more profoundly than ever before. However, power today is diffuse and it is shifting—mostly eastwards and southwards—in a manner that may prove as destabilizing as were the power shifts that came before the eruption of World War I.

Mounting friction between the big powers, particularly between Russia and the West, is perhaps the most perilous of all threats to the world—made all the more so by any lack of agreement on the status quo and how to change it. Russia sees the order that emerged from the Soviet Union's collapse as an unacceptable rejection of its great power status. The West sees Russia as revisionist. These tensions obstruct the work of the U.N. Security Council, whose dysfunction risks precipitating a crisis in global governance. This means that any local conflict, particularly in geostrategic areas like Ukraine or Syria, can provoke a dangerous escalation.

What does this gloomy picture mean for civil society groups working on building and sustaining peace?

Understanding conflict remains the starting point to resolving conflict. Field-based analysis has never been more vital: examining local dynamics and exploring the perspectives of all parties, including those perpetrating the violence and those who are suffering. Local analysis must now be paired with a good grasp of the roles of both the regional players and the big powers. Although fragmentation complicates diplomacy, it can present opportunities for creative partnerships. Only framework diplomacy, requiring different configurations for different conflicts and an intricate understanding of the interests and motives of all of the parties involved, stands any hope of ending the crises facing the world today.

Perhaps most importantly, we should persist in pressing those with power to do the right thing. War is never preordained. It is always a man-made disaster. In today's complex world, our compass must remain the commitment to the victims of war and to averting future tragedies. There is no excuse for ignorance and indifference.

7

The Real Danger Behind Cyberattacks

Scott D. Applegate

Scott D. Applegate is a United States Army information systems management officer with more than twenty-one years of experience. A published author and a frequent speaker at a number of security conferences, his current research interests include information assurance, cyberconflict, cybermilitias, security metrics, and cyberlaw.

Cyberattacks are a growing threat that too often go ignored or labeled as unrealistic danger. It is crucial for preventative measure to be put in place now. In the following piece, Scott Applegate explains that cybercrime does have a tangible impact on its victims and says, "Cyber attacks are often called non-violent or non-kinetic attacks, but the simple truth is that there is a credible capability to use cyber attacks to achieve kinetic effects."

Introduction

In the box office hit, *Live Free or Die Hard*, actor Bruce Willis takes on a group of cyber terrorists who begin systematically shutting down the United States by conducting cyber attacks and exploitation of critical infrastructure systems. In the midst of the movie, the main antagonist uses cyber attacks to inflict massive physical damage, injuries and death. While this kind of cyber inflicted mayhem currently remains in the realm of screenwriters and science fiction authors, the concept of inflicting physical damage, injury or death through Kinetic Cyber is no longer just

"The Dawn of Kinetic Cyber," by Scott D. Applegate, NATO CCD COE Publications, 2013. Reprinted by Permission.

a fictional construct of creative minds. Kinetic Cyber refers to a class of cyberattacks that can cause direct or indirect physical damage, injury or death solely though the exploitation of vulnerable information systems and processes. There have been a number of cyberattacks and laboratory experiments over the course of the last decade that foreshadow the dawn of kinetic cyber as the logical evolution of cyberwarfare.

Kinetic cyberattacks are a real and growing threat that is generally being ignored as unrealistic or alarmist. Regardless of the views of the doubters and naysayers, there is a growing body of evidence that shows kinetic cyber to be a valid and growing threat. These types of attacks have been validated experimentally in the laboratory environment, they have been used operationally in the context of espionage and sabotage, and they have been used criminally in a number of attacks throughout the world. It is imperative that the security community begin to take these types of threats seriously and address vulnerabilities associated with cyber physical systems and other devices that could be utilized to cause kinetic effects through cyberattacks.

Cyber Physical Systems

Generally, the main targets for kinetic cyberattacks are cyber physical systems (CPS). CPS refers to the tight conjoining of and coordination between computational and physical resources. CPS is the integration of computer systems with physical processes and its applications have the potential to dwarf the information technology revolution of the last few decades.[1] "The economic and societal potential of such systems is vastly greater than what has been realized, and major investments are being made worldwide to develop the technology."[1] CPS technologies are being integrated across a broad spectrum of industry sectors. These systems can be found in medical devices, traffic control and safety, advanced automotive systems, process control, energy conservation, environmental control, avionics, instrumentation, critical infrastructure control (electric power, water resources, and communications systems for example), distributed robotics, defense systems, manufacturing, and smart structures[1].

Unfortunately, like other information technologies, most were originally designed with little or no security, or security has been added after the fact. Many of these systems rely on the security-through-obscurity concept rather than building security into the design process. For example, of the 40 plus position papers presented at the National Science Foundation's Workshop on Cyber Physical Systems in 2006, only two actually focused on security aspects of CPS and these were more concerned with the networks that support these systems rather than the actual systems themselves.[2,3]

Furthermore, none of the presentations or working groups directly addressed the security requirements of these systems. CPS technologies are designed to have kinetic effects. They are designed to monitor and control physical processes through the use of computers and information technology. To a hacker or to someone who thinks outside-the-box, the mere fact of their existence and their interconnection to cyberspace implies that they could be manipulated and used for purposes other than those they were intended for. That is exactly what is happening. Hackers and security researchers are exploring the limits of these technologies and, as will be shown below, manipulating them to cause kinetic cybereffects both in the laboratory and in the real-world.

Validation of Kinetic Cyber

Cyberattacks are often called non-violent or non-kinetic attacks, but the simple truth is that there is a credible capability to use cyberattacks to achieve kinetic effects. Kinetic cyber attacks have been around for at least a decade and the ability to conduct these types of attacks has been validated in the laboratory environment through experimentation; in the operational environment to sabotage physical devices; and in the wild by hackers, hacktivists and other malicious actors.

[...]

The Future of Kinetic Cyber

Major investments, development and research are currently being conducted in the area of CPS and these types of systems are becoming more pervasive in industrialized states. The growth of CPS implies that the probability of seeing more kinetic cyberattacks targeting these types of systems is going to grow. Taking into account the types of attacks and research that has already occurred, it is not difficult to extrapolate the direction that kinetic cyber could take. The most dangerous avenue of growth would appear to be in the areas of SCADA, implantable medical devices, and automotive technologies although there are certainly other areas that are ripe for exploitation.

From the perspective of a nation-state, the ability to do serious damage to a rival state's critical infrastructure represents a strategic advantage. If an attack were able to successful damage a significant number of large electrical power plants in a manner similar to the Project Aurora experiment, the consequences could be economically destabilizing to the target state. Replacing the electrical generators in these types of plants can take months and cost millions of dollars per generator. In the meantime, the customers served by these plants would remain without power. Economist Scott Borg noted that if an attacker managed to knockout power to a third of the United States for a period of three months, the economy cost would be upwards of 700 billion dollars, which is the economic equivalent of 40 to 50 large hurricanes hitting at the same time.[5] This type of attack would be economically devastating and would have significant long-term consequences. While it is unlikely that a state would engage in this type of large-scale attack outside the bounds of an openly declared war, it would also be short-sighted to assume that only states will have access to these types of attacks.

Looking at the subversion of implantable medical devices or automobile control systems, these technologies could easily be exploited to injure or kill individuals or even groups of people. Such a use of kinetic cyber could be employed for murder or assassination of key figures. What makes this approach particularly insidious is that investigators would probably not realize there was a cyber component to these actions. Given the number of car accidents in a typical year, it is not beyond reason to assume that investigators would simply accept that a mechanical failure had caused a fatal accident rather that some form of cyberattack. This is especially true if the exploit leaves little or no residue of itself in the system after the fact. Since there have been no known incidents of cyberattacks causing car accidents, why would an investigator even suspect that this might be the case? The same is true of implantable medical devices. A recent article in Fire Engineering magazine points out that there is a possibility that arsonists may find a way in the near future to start fires using cyberattacks and that arson investigators would be highly unlikely to look for this as an underlying cause of a fire.[23] These types of incidents could be going on today and there is very little chance that they would be discovered.

The potential use of kinetic cyber by criminals or as a means of engaging in cyberwarfare is only limited by the ability of hackers and researchers to approach these technologies from an unconventional and innovative direction. These systems already have the capability to produce physical effects; it is therefore possible to subvert their functionality to do new and potentially dangerous tasks. Given the pervasive nature of network technology and the convergence of networked systems with cyber physical devices, these types of attacks are going to become far more common in the near future and the security community needs to begin addressing this problem now.

Addressing the Growing Threat

One of the first steps that should be taken in addressing the threat of kinetic cyber is to begin hardening CPS since these systems are often the main target of this type of attack. Security in CPS has followed the same trend that has been seen throughout the information technology industry. CPS devices were originally designed with little or no security. As a credible threat has emerged against CPS devices, designers and security researchers have begun to look at better ways to protect these vital systems. In 2012, the National Institute of Standards and Technology (NIST) held their first workshop on Cyber Physical Systems Security in Gaithersburg, Maryland. This was a two-day event with presentations and working groups focusing on a variety of industry areas such as smart power grids, SCADA, implantable medical devices and modern automobiles.

During the course of the NIST conference, a number of consistent themes emerged across all sectors of CPS. First and foremost was the need to create digitally signed and trusted instruction sets for cyber physical devices. Currently most CPS devices will accept instruction sets from any source so long as they have the correct format and syntax. This leaves devices highly vulnerable to exploitation through man-in-the-middle attacks and attacks which leverage packet injection such as those used in the CarShark experiment. Another suggested avenue of research involves the development of intrusion detection systems and reputation management systems for specific types of SCADA infrastructure such as smart power grids[24]. These types of security systems are vital in an environment where not all data that is received by a CPS device can be trusted.

[...]

Moving beyond technical solutions, it is important for policy makers, standards bodies, and governments to create reasonable and effective regulatory schemes to address security requirements in CPS. These devices are used in many sectors considered to be critical infrastructure. Industry has traditionally been resistant to new regulations and that will probably be the case with the CPS industries as well. That having been said, industry has the opportunity to take the initiative and voluntarily establish industry standards for security of CPS[25]. Doing so can serve to stave off overly restrictive efforts by government regulators and will allow the industry to shape the standards as they move forward. In additional to new regulatory schemes, governments and international bodies need to begin addressing kinetic cyber through diplomatic and legal efforts. Honest and open dialogue is needed in the international community to codify the definition of kinetic cyber and to establish thresholds for when these types of activities qualify as a use of force. Thus far, the international community has mostly avoided addressing cyber warfare and cyber conflict under the laws of armed conflict; however, the growing threat of kinetic cyber should spur new efforts to address these issues in a meaningful and thoughtful manner. It would be better to tackle this issue now, before a major kinetic cyber event happens, rather than trying to address the issue in the passion and turmoil that often follows such events.

These recommendations merely represent a good starting point for addressing the threat of kinetic cyber. There is a great deal of additional research that needs to be done to develop and implement technical solutions to address threats to CPS. In addition to technical solutions, policy makers, both domestically and in the international community, need to create common sense regulations for the CPS industry and begin to explore legal frameworks for codifying and addressing kinetic cyber.

[...]

References

1. E. A. Lee, "Cyber Physical Systems: Design Challenges," 2008 11th IEEE International Symposium on Object and Component-Oriented Real-Time Distributed Computing (ISORC), pp. 363–369, May 2008.

2. D. Kazakos, "Position Paper : Robust Communications Networks with Imbedded Security," in National Science Foundation on Cyber Physical Systems, 2006.

3. J. C. (Steve) Liu, "Secure plug and play architectures for cyber-physical systems A Position paper for the NSF workshop on cyber-physical systems," in National Science Foundation on Cyber Physical Systems, 2006.

4. A. Cui, M. Costello, and S. J. Stolfo, "When Firmware Modifications Attack : A Case Study of Embedded Exploitation," in 20th Annual Network & Distributed System Security Symposium, 2013.

5. J. Meserve, "US Sources : Staged cyber attack reveals vulnerability in power grid," Cable News Network, 26-Sep-2007. [Online]. Available: http://www.cnn.com/2007

US/09/26/power.at.risk/index.html. [Accessed: 30-Oct-2012].

6. L. Greenemeier, "Heart-Stopper : Could Hackers Hit Pacemakers , Other Medical Implants?," *Scientific American*, 14-Mar-2008.

7. D. Halperin, T. S. Heydt-Benjamin, K. Fu, T. Kohno, and W. H. Maisel, "Security and Privacy for Implantable Medical Devices," *IEEE Pervasive Computing*, vol. 7, no. 1, pp. 30–39, Jan. 2008.

8. B. Grubb, "Fatal risk at heart of lax security," *Sydney Morning Herald*, Sydney, Australia, 06-Nov-2012.

9. K. Koscher, A. Czeskis, F. Roesner, S. Patel, T. Kohno, S. Checkoway, D. McCoy, B. Kantor, D. Anderson, H. Shacham, and S. Savage, "Experimental Security Analysis of a Modern Automobile," in 2010 IEEE Symposium on Security and Privacy, 2010, pp. 447–462.

10. S. Checkoway and D. McCoy, "Comprehensive experimental analyses of automotive attack surfaces," in 20th USENIX Security Symposium, 2011.

11. M. Crawford, "Utility hack led to security overhaul," *Computerworld*, vol. 2006, pp. 1–2, 2006.

12. M. Abrams and J. Weiss, "Malicious Control System Cyber Security Attack Case Study – Maroochy Water Services, Australia," in NIST Industrial Process Control System Workshop, 2008.

13. T. Smith, "Hacker jailed for revenge sewage attacks Job rejection caused a bit of a stink," *The Register*, 31-Oct-2001.

14. S. Hymon, "Engineers, Architects Strike Out on Picket Lines," *Los Angeles Times*, Los Angeles, California, 11-Sep-2006.

15. S. Bernstein and A. Blankstein, "Key signals targeted, officials say," *Los Angeles Times*, Los Angeles, California, 09-Jan-2007.

16. M. Krasnowski, "2 men accused of hacking into traffic system," *San Diego Union-Tribune*, San Diego, CA, 21-Jan-2007.

17. S. Grad, "Engineers who hacked into L.A. traffic signal computer, jamming streets, sentenced," *Los Angeles Times*, Los Angeles, California, 01-Dec-2009.

18. J. Leyden, "Polish teen derails tram after hacking train network," *The Register*, 11-Jan-2008.

19. G. Baker, "Schoolboy hacks into city's tram system," *The Telegraph*, 11-Jan-2008.

20. A. Matrosov, E. Rodionov, D. Harley, and J. Malcho, "Stuxnet under the microscope," 2010.

21. D. Albright, P. Brannan, and C. Walrond, "Did Stuxnet Take Out 1,000 Centrifuges at the Natanz Enrichment Plant ?," Washington D.C., 2010.

22. A. Bloom, "60 Minutes - Stuxnet: Computer worm opens new era of warfare," CBS News, 2012.

23. K. Coleman, "Arson by Cyber Attack," Fire Engineering, 12-Dec-2012. [Online]. Available: http://www.fireengineering.com/articles/2012/12/arson-by-cyber attack. html. [Accessed: 18-Dec-2012].

24. R. Moreno, "Cyber-Physical Systems Security for the Smart Grid," in Cybersecurity in Cyber-Physical Systems Workshop, 2012.

25. A. Weimerskirch, "Safety-Critical Automotive and Industrial Data Security (Extended Abstract)," in Cybersecurity in Cyber-Physical Systems Workshop, 2012.

26. M. Ben Salem, "Security Challenges and Requirements for Control Systems in the Semiconductor Manufacturing Sector (Extended Abstract)," in Cybersecurity in Cyber-Physical Systems Workshop, 2012, pp. 1–3.

27. S. Gupta, "Implantable Medical Devices - Cyber Risks and Mitigation Approaches," in Cybersecurity in Cyber-Physical Systems Workshop, 2012.

8

How Malware Hides in Plain Sight

Henry S. Kenyon

Data privacy reporter and analyst Henry S. Kenyon writes about the interconnections between government, business and technology, with a focus on the defense industry and trends in electronics, IT systems, robotics, weapons systems and aerospace. He has written for CQ Roll Call, Aerospace America, Signal *magazine as well as other publications.*

The dramatic increase in phishing and malware attacks over the past decade is linked to economic gain. Hackers are now often paid to invade personal and corporate information through a variety of unexpected ways "Focused, sophisticated attacks target specific users, concentrate on social networking sites," notes Henry Kenyon as a lead-in to the following piece, in which he details the various types of attacks and what can be done to combat them. Education and antivirus defense, he says, is key.

S trategic efforts to access top executives' computers and to steal source code and intellectual property are taking cybercrime beyond simple financial theft. Criminals and foreign organizations are launching more sophisticated and targeted phishing and malware attacks, resulting in more prevalent infiltrations in 2009. Cybercriminals often target social media sites, such as Twitter and

"Cybercriminals Find New Ways to Exploit Vulnerabilities," by Henry S. Kenyon, AFCEA International, March 2010. Reprinted by Permission.

Facebook, and use an individual's personal data to fool friends and colleagues into revealing valuable personal and corporate data.

A white paper called the "Cyber Intelligence Report" published by Cyveillance, a subsidiary of QinetiQ North America, covers the last half of 2008 and the first half of 2009, but the report's author, Eric Olson, Cyveillance's vice president of solutions assurance, maintains that the documented trends remained constant throughout the latter half of 2009. One trend that continued from 2008 was a drop in phishing attacks, but he warns that criminals have simply revised their methods and shifted from mass mailing efforts to well-researched and very specific attacks. Olson notes that the number of malicious software and phishing attempts are underreported, as is the level of malicious Web pages and attempts to access user information through social engineering and other methods. He adds that a variety of lures are used, ranging from pornography, malicious pay-per-click links to tweets with embedded links.

Chief among the report's findings was that antivirus software provides limited protection against malware. The study measured the effectiveness of 13 major antivirus vendors in real time. It found that even the most popular products detected less than half of the malware threats. Olson describes antivirus and firewall systems as "fixed emplacements" in the battle against viruses and hacking. Although such defenses are necessary, he explains that they are not sufficient because they are reactive to these threats. The best defense is for users to be educated and aware of trends in online criminal activity, he says.

Browser antiphishing systems also have difficulty detecting most attacks when they are launched. The report notes that attack detection rates improve significantly after 24 hours, but adds that the majority of the damage caused by phishing takes place in the first 24 hours. Olson contends that one reason for this detection delay is that the malware's writers also own copies of the antivirus software and know how to counter it.

Malware distribution continues to be a growing trend. The report divides malware into a fraud chain consisting of hosting sites, distribution sites and drop sites. Malware hosting sites store and deliver their binary files to malware distribution sites. According to the report, the majority of malware hosting locations are in the United States and China, with the two nations combined representing 52 percent of the global total. Criminals favor the United States as their target for hosting and compromising computers because of the nation's high user population, Olson shares.

The United States and China also were the two top malware distributors, with the United States in the lead. Criminals use a variety of methods to attract unwary visitors to sites where their computers can be infected. The report notes that distribution sites are usually targeted at specific types of Internet users. Germany is the leading host country for malware drop sites used to collect information from computers infected with keyloggers, screen scrapers and other programs used to gather personal data passively. Olson adds that hackers and malware distributors no longer bother to use servers in their own countries. "They are simply compromising other people's Web sites or home computers, 'botting' them and turning them into the Web server," he says.

Spreading malware usually begins with a lure, most often a compromised legitimate Web site serving as a vector. Other types of lures can range from authoritative e-mails from a high-level member of a government agency or company whose name has been pulled off the Internet, instant messages or tweets with embedded links. "The idea is to have some compelling way to get a link in front of users that they will click on," Olson says.

When a malicious site is visited, the page will execute code attempting to install the malware. Olson notes that such sites can be hosted by a legitimate organization while the malware being pushed into a computer is hosted in China, or vice versa. "The Web site you visit is not necessarily—in fact it's quite often not—the Web site that actually drops the malware. The site that you visit is, more often than not, a legitimate site that's been compromised by the bad guys," he says.

A recent example of a trusted Web site being used to distribute malicious code involved the *New York Times* home page. Criminals legitimately bought pay-per-click advertisements and used them to lead users to malicious sites. Olson notes that the newspaper had no influence over the material placed in the banners. The false ads were placed around a specific article and were tailored to attract people who had read the story. After the incident, the *Times* had to apologize to its users. "Even though they had nothing to do with it—they were technologically blameless—it didn't help their business any," he relates.

Malware can be propagated through a variety of methods. Although it is now relatively rare, malicious attachments are still used, but criminals have become more sophisticated and selective about whom they target. These types of researched, specific attacks are spear phishing. "While the e-mail vector is a much smaller percentage than it used to be, the cases where it does appear are increasingly targeted at members of specific agencies, specific lines of work, specific professional organizations and the like," he observes.

One example of a spear phishing attack involved a number of corporate chief executive officers (CEOs), including the CEO of Cyveillance. The victims received a detailed e-mail disguised as a court summons citing their names, titles, types of business and the address to the district court closest to their headquarters. The letter notified the CEOs that their companies were being sued for an offense that was credible to their specific businesses. The letter then indicated that to view the complaint or subpoena, the recipient should open the attached PDF file. "This was something that was clearly targeted at getting access to specific executives' computers via malicious attachment," he says.

Another type of attack is a malicious Web page that exploits a vulnerability in a browser to conduct a "drive-by download." The very act of visiting these pages will activate malware that will attempt to install on the user's computer. But not all malware is an installed application. Olson notes that an increasing amount of malware runs directly in the browser window in non-executable code. When a user closes the browser, the code is gone—there is nothing in the user's computer, the malware just runs in the browser. He notes that antivirus software has yet to catch up with these trends because there are so many weaknesses in browsers, PDFs and other legitimate programs that criminals can exploit. (See sidebar above for an antivirus vendor's view of the situation.)

Criminals also can use social engineering to convince a user to accept a download voluntarily. Olson notes that forums and message boards are now filled with automated postings of pornographic thumbnails. Once a person has clicked on the link, it will indicate that they must download a media player to watch the video and to click onto the link to allow the installation. He notes that in these cases, users actually allow their machines to be compromised by an executable application. Other examples include advertisements for downloadable programs to animate mouse cursors or screen backgrounds that serve as a front for additional material being installed on a computer. "It's 3 k [kilobytes] of code to turn your cursor into a kitty cat and the other six megabytes is all malware," he relates.

Phishing is a social engineering technique that combines technology and human interaction to gather personal data for fraud and identity theft. The report found that while phishing attacks dropped to 23,000 per month in the first half of 2009, down from 36,000 per month in the second half of 2008, the attacks themselves have become more sophisticated.

Among its findings, the report indicated that while banks and credit unions remain the major targets of phishing attacks, criminals now are focusing on government and commercial organizations. Social networking sites are quickly becoming a target of choice because of the amount of personal data that can be accessed. Olson notes that social networking "takes social engineering to a new level of sophistication, and unfortunately, ease."

Large-scale spamming and even relatively narrowly targeted phishing and malware attacks still must get past the intended victim's initial mistrust of receiving a message from a stranger. Olson explains that hackers phish a variety of sites with no monetary value because if they can recover a password or other personal information, it provides criminals with tools to access a person's social and business contacts.

Once hackers have a user's password, considerable damage can be done, Olson says. He notes that seven out of 10 times, most people use the same password for multiple sites. By accessing a person's e-mail account, criminals can approach a person's friends and relatives in the guise of that person. This is because the sender now appears to be from inside the recipient's circle of trust or acquaintance. Because of this trust, Olson asserts that the infection and victimization rate of compromised personal information is much higher. "That social networking context means that once a user's account or device is compromised, that user's network is at extremely high risk. An inherent circle of trust exists around that user, and most people fail to distinguish from the user and their device or their account," he says.

Olson explains that while social networking is a great tool, it also leverages what he sees as the underlying vulnerability of the Internet in terms of transparency, efficiency and instantaneous connectivity to anyone anywhere. "You have just about no way to know that anyone is whom he or she claims to be, because what you're counting on is that the account or login or device equates to the person, and that isn't necessarily true," he says.

Financial fraud is another major target for malware. Olson notes that this is attractive to criminals because it is relatively easy to access people's financial data. However, small-time financial crime is not his key concern. Olson's greatest fears are incidents such as the Chinese malware attack propagated through malicious PDF attachments that sought out source code and intellectual property from more than 30 major companies with operations in

China. These companies included Hewlett-Packard, Apple, Yahoo! and Google.

The same group behind this first attack also was linked to PDFs sent to defense contractors planning to attend a conference in Las Vegas. "To me, that says they're after source code; they're after intellectual property; they're after people who work in the defense industry. Frankly, I'd rather deal with guys who are just up to robbing banks because this [theft of intellectual property] smacks of someone with a much more strategic agenda," he says.

Education a Key Defense Against Cyberthreats

The past year has seen an increase in sophisticated malware and online scams. These trends in cybercriminal activity will continue in 2010, says Keith Rhodes, senior vice president and chief technology officer for the Mission Solutions Group of QinetiQ North America. He explains that a broader challenge for organizations is that passive network defenses are inadequate because malware and other types of attacks are outmaneuvering firewalls and intrusion detection systems. The pace of software and hacker toolkit development has become highly automated. "It's almost a production line approach," Rhodes says.

A key factor is that malware and phishing are moneymaking criminal enterprises. "This is no longer just trying to get your hacker bona fides. This is now a business," he says. Because of the money involved, cybercrime moves at a pace relevant to the environment.

The best defense, Rhodes maintains, is to be educated about cyberthreats. "You have to be an active participant in protecting yourself, which means you have to look at what's going on out there in the wild, away from yourself and as close to a source as you can get," he says. For example, chief information officers who are worried about the criminal element in Eastern Europe should actively study trends and events there. Education and awareness of threats applies to all users. "You are absolutely an active participant in looking at the world and what is going on there," he says.

Rhodes says that last year's increase in browser-based attacks and online fraud will continue, if not increase. Another factor is that these attacks now require less active cooperation from users to have malware payloads inserted into their computers. "It's requiring less participation on the victim's part in order to have the system be corrupted, which means that the user population has to have a much more active role in protecting itself, and you protect yourself primarily with knowledge," he says.

"As with lots of things, the defenders have to be right 100 percent of the time, and the adversaries have to be right once. That is the struggle. In cyber, the adversary has the upper hand because there is so much software, infrastructure and equipment out there that is at varying levels of sophistication and protection that the adversary doesn't have to go directly against a person or organization, he can go against someone who is connected to the target but isn't as well protected," he says.

Security providers understand that they are challenged by real-time threats, Rhodes explains. In response, these firms are providing more tailored offerings for their customers. Vendors now are conducting risk analysis of organizations and trying to create more analytical capabilities. However, the challenge is that these responses must be tailored to an organization's specific needs.

Antivirus Defenses Must Be Agile to Counter Malware Threats

The Cyveillance Cyber Intelligence Report for 2009 indicates that antivirus vendors' products, while important, are not completely effective against malware and other sophisticated online threats. David Markus, director of security research and communications at McAfee Labs, agrees with some of the report's key assumptions about the rise in malware attacks and their financial focus, but believes that antivirus products are more effective than the report indicates. Some of the varying results come from the way the testing is done, he allows.

"Standard antivirus technology is kind of passé at this point in time because threats are complex," Markus says. Because the threats are so varied, he emphasizes that McAfee does not offer simple signature-based malware recognition systems but rather a range of flexible technologies such as host-based intrusion prevention systems and white listing technologies.

Speaking for McAfee, Markus notes that gathering intelligence about cyberthreats is vital for antivirus vendors. This data is embedded into each new generation of the firm's antivirus and network protection technologies at a variety of levels. He adds that mitigating threats at the appropriate layer in the network is the key for future network and antivirus systems. "The bad guys are smart. They're good at testing against security products. That's kind of the one-up they have on us good guys. They can create testbeds with all of our technologies in them and run samples against every single [antivirus] technology and adjust it," he says. However, he adds that firms such as McAfee with a breadth of global intelligence and research experience can insert defenses across all layers of a network.

Because criminals take advantage of weaknesses in browsers and network architecture, Markus explains that antivirus vendors must be agile. This flexibility includes conducting research across a variety of technologies and security applications. However, he notes, detection and response to malware and virus attacks is not perfect. "There's always going to be that person who runs across that site or that piece of malware for the first time," he says. But he guarantees that such new threats are quickly collected, analyzed and the appropriate patches or defenses then are distributed to users.

9

The Ambiguity of Cyberwarfare in Law

Ido Kilovaty

Ido Kilovaty is a research scholar in law, a cyber fellow at the Center for Global Legal Challenges, and a resident fellow at the Information Society Project at Yale Law School. His research focuses on international law and cyberspace, and he's assisting in developing a cross-disciplinary project on cyberconflict.

International Humanitarian Law (IHL)—like the Geneva Conventions, which were adopted by the international community in 1949—was created to protect civilians from armed groups, military objectives, and large attacks. When it comes to cyberwarfare however, what counts as an attack is not always clear-cut. In the following piece, Ido Kilovaty talks about the various implications of cyberdisruptions and asserts that, "the law is still in an inadequate position in addressing the myriad challenges of cyberconflict."

It is already widely acknowledged that cyberspace has become the fifth domain of warfare, and militaries around the world are training various cyberunits, who will be supporting military operations, both by defending cyberinfrastructure, and by engaging in cyberattacks, with the purpose of manipulating, interrupting, and damaging the computer systems and networks of the enemy. While technological developments allow warring sides to employ sophisticated means and methods of warfare, they also pose a host

"Violence in Cyberspace: Are Disruptive Cyberspace Operations Legal under International Humanitarian Law?" by Ido Kilovaty, *Just Security*, March 03, 2017. Reprinted by Permission.

of new challenges with regard to civilians and civilian objects, who may become susceptible to the new adverse effects of conflict. One example would be cyberoperations that cause massive disruption —whether they target the electric grid, the Internet infrastructure, or civilian communications.

In general terms, international humanitarian law (known as IHL, but often referred to in the U.S. as the law of armed conflict) protects civilians from attacks. The most basic rule of IHL makes it illegal to directly attack civilians, unless and for such time as they directly participate in hostilities. This notion of distinction is one of the core values that the whole corpus of international humanitarian law is based on. According to international humanitarian law, legitimate targets of attacks are combatants, members of armed groups, and other military objectives. While it is generally accepted that international humanitarian law applies to cyberspace operations, it is not always clear whether a specific cyberoperation falls within the legal definition of "attacks." "Attacks" is a legal term of art, defined by Additional Protocol I of the Geneva Conventions (AP I) as "acts of violence against the adversary, whether in offence or in defence." Essentially, the key to understanding whether a particular cyberspace operation directed at civilians is legal or not, is asking whether it is an "*attack*," in other words, if it constitutes an "act of violence."

As I argued in a new paper in the *Michigan Telecommunications and Technology Law Review*, a disruption can indeed qualify as "violence" in cyberspace, a view that is at odds with the recent *Tallinn Manual 2.0 on the International Law Applicable to Cyber Operations*, and its treatment of this matter.

IHL Protects Civilians from Disruption

After looking at a "disruption" as the primary harm resulting from a cyberoperation, the most intuitive argument is that IHL already protects civilians from disruptive cyber operations. This argument is primarily based on interpreting the term "violence" using the regular process of treaty interpretation, as provided by the Vienna Convention on the Law of Treaties (VCLT). The VCLT establishes that terms within a treaty shall be understood by their "ordinary meaning." Therefore, "violence" should be interpreted by referring to its regular definition, which happens to be broader than simple exhibition of physical force, and also includes "intimidation," "great intensity or severity… of something undesirable," and the French definition also defines violence as "physical or moral constraint." Violence is a broad enough concept, that "attacks" is deemed to protect civilians from a broad range of military operations, whether they cause physical harm, or they result in massive disruption effects.

In addition, IHL has several hints in its respective texts, implying that civilians are in fact protected from many potential threats. For example, civilians are protected from "*dangers* arising from military operations" and from "Acts or threats of violence the primary purpose of which is to spread terror among the civilian population." IHL also requires that adversaries "direct their *operations* only against military objectives" and that "in the conduct of military operations, constant care shall be taken to spare the civilian population" In that context, "military operations" are defined rather broadly as "all the movements and activities carried out by armed forces related to hostilities." This, in a way, provides the context, object, and purpose of IHL.

While the *Tallinn Manual 2.0* agrees that violence is not limited to kinetic force, it still holds the view that cyberattacks are to be understood as resulting in "violent effects," that "cause injury or death to persons or damage or destruction to objects" thereby excluding "psychological cyberoperations and cyberespionage." It is also evident that the Manual's experts overemphasized the physicality factor. For example, the Manual addresses cyberoperations that interfere with "the functionality of an object," concluding that this would be an "attack" only if restoring the functionality would require the replacement of physical components, though some experts argued that the reinstallation of a software or restitution of data would also qualify.

Tallinn Manual 2.0 and Disruptive Cyberoperations

The *Tallinn Manual 2.0* does an interesting move in terms of disruptive cyberoperations. Methodically, the Manual intends to identify *lex lata*—the law as it is at present, which restricts the ability of the Manual to expand certain legal concepts in light of the challenges presented by cyberoperations. An example is the Manual's treatment of cyberoperations with large-scale disruptive effects, such as "disrupting all email communications throughout the country". The Manual confessed that there is "logic in characterising [this type of] operation as an attack" but that IHL "does not presently extend this far". This is identical to the previous *Tallinn Manual*, or in other words—no change.

This leads to a somewhat bizarre result, for instance, whereas in a scenario where a cyberoperation necessitates hardware replacement would require the attacker to comply with the principle of distinction (and other IHL norms), that would not be the case if a target's e-mail communications were to be shut down entirely due to a cyberoperation, or by analogy, access to the Internet as a whole. This narrow reading of "violence" is not in line with the humanitarian purposes IHL is trying to achieve. This includes limiting adverse effects of armed conflicts, allowing military operations *only* against military objectives, and protecting civilians from direct attacks. Rather, it puts civilians and civilian objects under threat of disruptive cyberoperations, which will be used as a form of "unduly coercion," namely, a form of legitimate targeting of civilians for the purpose of leverage against the opposing adversary.

Redrawing the Line Between Violence and Non-Violence

The *Tallinn Manual 2.0* is limited by its methodology and absence of normative authority. This simply illustrates that the law is still in an inadequate position in addressing the myriad challenges of cyberconflict. The Manual acknowledges that should "such [disruptive] cyberoperations break out, the international community would generally regard them as attack," this is perhaps the closest the Manual could get to saying that the law should develop in a way that recognizes the threat of large-scale disruptions.

Thomas Rid, author of "Cyber War Will Not Take Place," says that cyberspace is leading us to rethink the idea of violence and how to protect against it. He contends that this requires us to redraw the line currently drawn between violence and non-violence, something the Manual fails to do. Nils Melzer, then legal adviser to the ICRC, exemplified the difficulty of avoiding the question of line drawing—"it would hardly be convincing to exclude the non-destructive incapacitation of a state's air defense system or other critical military infrastructure from the notion of attack simply because it does not directly cause death, injury or destruction." This, I believe, also extends to non-destructive operations targeting civilians. At the end of the day, States are responsible for reshaping the notion of violence in cyberspace, and the *Tallinn Manual 2.0* alludes to it by deferring that question to the international community.

Conclusion

The digital era leads to an increase in the weight of certain values, such as data and global connectivity, while decreasing the relative importance and cost of physical objects. This should encourage us to rethink what ought to be protected, and incorporate it within the law. Disruption, in that context, is something an information society cannot tolerate, particularly when directed against civilians and civilian objects. That could be just as violent as destruction, if not more. Hopefully, the international community and organizations will spearhead this evolution.

10

Governing Cyberweapons

Tim Stevens

Dr. Tim Stevens joined King's College London as a lecturer in global security in September 2016. His research looks at global security practices in cybersecurity and digital surveillance. He has also written on time and temporality in international relations theory, most recently in Cyber Security and the Politics of Time *from Cambridge University Press.*

Cyberweapons and their consequences are a contemporary problem, the solutions for which are still being explored. Instead of allowing individual governments to handle the problem, there should be a push for global governance—a transnational approach to cybersecurity and what to do when crimes are committed. According to the following academic paper by Tim Stevens, this will prevent power from falling into the hands of individual governments and instead engage a worldwide effort.

Abstract

Cyberweapons are a relatively new addition to the toolbox of contemporary conflict but have the potential to destabilize international relations. Since Stuxnet (a malicious computer worm) in 2010 demonstrated how computer code could be weaponised to generate political effect, cyberweapons have increasingly been discussed in terms of potential regulation and prohibition. Most analyses focus on how global institutions and regimes might be

"Cyberweapons: an emerging global governance architecture", by Tim Stevens, Palgrave Macmillan, January 10, 2017. http://www.nature.com/articles/palcomms2016102 Licensed under CC BY 4.0.

developed to regulate the development and use of cyberweapons and identify the political and technical obstacles to fulfilling this ambition. This focus on centralized authority obscures identification of existing governance efforts in this field, which together constitute an emerging global governance architecture for offensive cyber capabilities. This article explores three sources of cyberweapons governance—cyberwarfare, cybercrime and export controls on dual-use technologies—and briefly describes their political dynamics and prospects. It is argued that although fragmented, the global governance of cyberweapons should not be dismissed on this basis. Fragmentation is a condition of global governance, not its antithesis, and policy should respect this fragmentation instead of regarding it as an impediment to further development of cyberweapons governance. This article is published as part of a collection on global governance.

Introduction

Cyberweapons have been covert military and intelligence tools since the 1990s but it was only in 2010 that the strategic potential of weaponised code was put under the global spotlight. The disclosure by technical experts and journalists of a cyberweapon dubbed "Stuxnet" showed how computer code could be weaponised to generate political effect. Reportedly the product of a highly-classified US-Israeli intelligence programme, Stuxnet infiltrated the control systems of an Iranian nuclear facility to subvert its uranium enrichment operations (Sanger, 2012: 188–225; Zetter, 2014). It succeeded in doing so and, although its impact on the Iranian nuclear programme is probably overstated (Barzashka, 2013), it demonstrated that cyberweapons could be deployed as political weapons in pursuit of national interests. Stuxnet has also reopened older debates about how, and if, the acquisition and use of cyberweapons should be regulated or even prohibited, through institutions like "cyber arms control" regimes and conventions. This work suggests that obstacles to building such institutions are significant and possibly counter-productive and perhaps should not be attempted in the first place. The continued focus on centralized mechanisms has prevented a clear assessment of extant or emerging measures regulating the acquisition and use of cyberweapons in peace and war. This commentary proposes that global governance is a more appropriate lens through which to view these processes and that a nascent global governance architecture for cyberweapons already exists.

Cyberweapons

"Cyberweapon" has become a catch-all term for diverse forms of malicious software (malware) for which an extraordinary range of capabilities is claimed. Cyberweapons are conceived on a spectrum from low-level internet irritants, to war-winning "cyberbombs," even to the equivalents of "weapons of mass destruction." The reality is rather less dramatic and the term—if it is to be used at all (Valeriano et al., 2016)—has been defined as "computer code that is used, or designed to be used, with the aim of threatening or causing physical, functional, or mental harm to structures, systems, or living beings" (Rid and McBurney, 2012; Rid, 2013: 37). This is broadly analogous to established notions of a weapon as "an offensive capability that is applied, or that is intended or designed to be applied, to an adversary to cause death, injury or damage" (Boothby, 2016: 166). However, these are not juridical or legal terms, as there is no consensus definition of either weapons or cyberweapons in international law. For our purposes, it is sufficient that a weapon meets the criteria of intentionality and harm, although cyberweapons present at least two additional challenges to definition and conceptualization.

The first is that most cyberweapons lack conventional physicality: they are computer code that exists only in information infrastructures like the internet. They are "in the world but not experienced as part of the world" (Floridi, 2014: 318), until such time as their effects manifest in more conventional ways. The existence, operations and effects of cyberweapons and other "information objects" are wholly contingent on physical processes, entities and events (Dipert, 2014: 36–37), but cyberweapons are not themselves physical in any natively comprehensible fashion. This is significant, not only as this makes them difficult to track and interdict, but because most jurisdictions and legal regimes understand weapons to be material, rather than immaterial, entities (Mele, 2013: 9). The exception to this is when modified hardware is used as a cyberweapon, or when hardware is specifically designed to be part of a cyberweapons system (Schmitt, 2013: 142), both of which should be considered alongside cyberweapons *qua* informational objects.

The second is the nature of harm. Moral arguments as to the nature of harm—most notably in the liberal tradition (Linklater, 2006)—do not consider harm to non-humans, so the extension of the concept of harm to "structures, systems, or living beings" (Rid, 2013: 37) is philosophically problematic (also, Arimatsu, 2012: 97). "Harm" in this context must include the related concepts of "damage" or "impairment", which do apply to non-humans and non-sentient systems. In a slightly metaphorical register, therefore, this expansive category of harm covers outcomes injurious to the well-being of a target system, or which set back the interests of that system. For example, malware that extracts data but does not use it to degrade or subvert a computer system would not be considered a cyberweapon (Rid, 2013: 47). However, as establishing the nature and degree of harm is a notoriously subjective process, it is difficult to develop precise thresholds for what constitutes harm or otherwise, not least as the type and severity of harm depends on the nature of the target. Notwithstanding the issue of whether non-cognising entities can experience harm, this points to the relational nature of harm. Cyberweapons are not equipped with "an explosive charge", so harm is caused by altering processes of the targeted system, rather than as a direct result of some innate attribute of weaponised code (Rid, 2013: 41). This applies to the logical functioning of a targeted computer system, which is affected directly by a cyberweapon, and to the second-order effects of cyberweaponry, such as financial loss or reputational damage to a company subject caused by a cyberattack. It should also include the affective implications of the use of cyberweapons (Stevens,

2016a: 103–104) if they result in harm, perceived or actual, to human subjects. These might include feelings of insecurity or fear caused by infrastructure failure, or the more mundane but no less real emotions that result from personal data loss. In both cases, these are usually indirect weapons effects (Rid, 2013: 40), although, *contra* Rid, this does not necessarily alter the original code's intended status as a weapon.

One further comment is necessary on the identification of software as a weapon. As the above discussion affirms, weapons are not technical artefacts alone but hybrid assemblages of human and non-human entities (Bourne, 2012). The appeals to harm and intent reflect this concern with human agency as the principal determinant of "weapon-ness" throughout the various stages of planning, design, development and deployment, as well as in mechanisms of commercial and criminal exchange. Nevertheless, the construction of malware as weapons may on occasion hinder rather than help understanding of these complex entities. This operates, first, by conflating disparate tools and instruments within a single rubric and, second, by masking the heterogeneity of their anatomies and deployments within a field of militarized discursivity. As we will encounter below in the discussion of dual-use technologies, many "cyberweapons" have defensive rather than offensive purposes, and, far from being intended to cause harm, can be used for socially beneficial reasons. In that instance, malware would cease to be a weapon *per se*, but this does demonstrate the inherently fuzzy boundaries between which instance of software constitutes a weapon and which does not. "Cyberweapon" is retained here, both because it is tightly if imperfectly defined herein, but also because it provides an opportunity to engage with the substantial literature that already uses the term. It is hoped that future work can develop a more productive and nuanced terminology.

Cyberweapons and global governance

Stuxnet was widely perceived as a "game-changer" in international affairs (Farwell and Rohozinski, 2011, 2012; Collins and McCombie,

2012) by demonstrating the political potential of cyberweapons, which, like all weapons, aim to change the behaviour of an adversary. The reputed subsequent online publication of portions of the Stuxnet code sparked fears of proliferation to non-state actors including terrorists, and the possibility of an inter-state cyber "arms race" (Singer and Friedman, 2014: 158–159; Craig and Valeriano, 2016; Limnéll, 2016). Stuxnet also reinvigorated a long-running discussion about if cyberweapons should be regulated and which parties might be capable of doing so. Early authors on the topic pointed out that non-state use of cyberweapons might be subject to criminal law, and state use by international humanitarian law, but that any regime would be of limited use without significant international commitments to monitoring, verification, compliance and enforcement (Denning, 2000, 2001; Sofaer and Goodman, 2000). States would also be resistant to cyber arms control measures if they restricted their capacity to respond to aggression, by states or non-state actors, although they might help promote norms around offensive cyberweapons use (Eriksson, 1999; Rathmell, 2003).

Subsequent analyses have tended to default to one of two frames in discussing the regulation of cyberweapons. The first is arms control, in which historical experiences with nuclear, biological and chemical weapons serve as resources for thinking through how arms control mechanisms might be applied to cyberweapons (Brown, 2006; Geers, 2010; Meyer, 2011; Arimatsu, 2012; Maybaum and Tölle, 2016). The second frame concerns the criminalization of cyberweapons (Denning, 2000, 2001; Prunckun, 2008), drawing on the evolution of the Council of Europe Convention on Cybercrime (2001), discussed in greater detail below. In both frames, there is a presumption towards globally binding legal mechanisms administered by a central, hierarchical authority and supported by leading powers, the absence of either portending the likely failure of attempts to regulate or prohibit cyberweapons. What is missing from this literature is an attempt to look at cyberweapons governance "in the round", understood as a concern with what currently exists, rather than what might be future optimal solutions

(Stevens, 2016b). Specifically, the cyberweapons literature, in its concern with legal and institutional *regimes*, does not address the importance of *global governance* frameworks for understanding international politics.

Emerging at the end of the Cold War and cognisant of the growing potency of globalization, "global governance" represented an interdisciplinary concern with international order in a post-bipolar world (Zumbansen, 2012: 84). In International Relations (IR), this translated into understanding order as having foundations other than traditional political-legal authority, including the roles of transnational and non-state actors, and in finding positive solutions to transnational problems (Hofferberth, 2015: 601). As Coen and Pegram (2015) observe, recent IR global governance scholarship has moved beyond a narrow focus on multilateral institutions and great powers to incorporate the agency of diverse actors and constituencies. One analytical framework emerging from this work is that of "global governance architectures."

A "global governance architecture" is "the overarching system of public and private institutions, principles, norms, regulations, decision-making procedures and organizations that are valid or active in a given issue area of world politics" (Biermann et al., 2009). This framework is narrower in scope than "order," which speaks to the organization of international relations in general, but broader than "regime," which tends towards a focus on institutions (Biermann et al., 2009: 15–16). Global governance architectures consist of vertically fragmented arrangements of multilevel governance (subnational, national, international, supranational) and horizontally fragmented multipolar governance structures of state and non-state actors (Biermann and Pattberg, 2012: 13). The making and implementation of rules is located at multiple points in this matrix, although interlinkages between the various layers and poles of authority and practice are necessary to translate rules and policies from one locus to another. The potential utility of this analytical framework to global cyberweapons governance is currently unexplored. As a first step, the following section identifies existing attempts to regulate cyberweapons in the fields of cyberwarfare, cybercrime, and export controls on dual-use technologies. Each field of activity attempts to regulate a different aspect of cyberweapons acquisition or use. Cyberwarfare is concerned with the use of cyberweapons in war; cybercrime with the acquisition and use of information technologies that can be used in the prosecution of crime by non-state actors; export controls aim to prevent transfer and proliferation of dual-use technologies that can be used to develop or facilitate cyber weapons use by state and non-state actors.

Sources of cyberweapons governance

Cyberwarfare is subject to significant attention presently and one key task is to ascertain how it articulates with international humanitarian law (*jus in bello*). The most comprehensive attempt thus far is the Tallinn Manual Process (TMP), based at the NATO Cooperative Cyber Defence Centre of Excellence (CCD COE) in Estonia. The *Tallinn Manual on the International Law Applicable to Cyber Warfare* (*Tallinn Manual*), an exhaustive analysis by international lawyers, finds that customary international law applies to cyberwarfare, as with other forms of military force (Schmitt, 2013). The *Tallinn Manual* addresses cyberweapons within this framework, suggesting that they are prohibited from causing "unnecessary suffering" to combatants if military objectives are not furthered by their use (Schmitt, 2013: 143). Noncombatants are already protected in law and should not be subject to cyberweapons use. The TMP has no binding legal status but NATO formally incorporated its recommendations into its Enhanced Cyber Defence Policy (NATO 2014: article 72). The United Kingdom has confirmed these principles in defence strategy (Ministry of Defence, 2013), as has the United States (US Department of Defense, 2015a). US military doctrine for cyberwarfare also respects *opinio juris* on the matter, although submits that "[p]recisely how the law of war applies to cyber operations is not well-settled" (US Department of

Defense, 2015b: 996), a situation the second volume of the *Tallinn Manual* will address in late 2016 (NATO CCD COE, 2015).

Russia asserts that the TMP serves the bellicose interests of "the West," whereas Russia prefers "a diametrically opposed policy of averting military and political confrontations in information space" (Krutskikh and Streltsov, 2014: 75). Both propositions are rejected by one TMP expert, who surmises that Russia criticizes the TMP because it "run[s] counter to their objective of modelling international law in a manner that serves the interests of the Russian Federation" (von Heinegg, 2015: 2). Neither the Russian claim nor the NATO rebuttal is unjustified: law is as much about facilitation as it is about prohibition. When law is translated into military doctrine, doctrine is an enabler of military operations. It constrains actions in important ways but provides opportunities in others. The TMP and any corresponding processes seek to preserve and maximize military freedom of movement in pursuit of political goals, congruent with particular interpretations of international law and prevailing norms. It follows that the legitimacy and modes of cyberweapons deployment in war depend on how divergent national and coalition interests are translated into laws, norms and, perhaps, future treaties.

The debate about cyberweapons and cyberwarfare rests on the interpretation of existing international law and its applicability to a novel weapons class. In contrast, discussions about global cybercrime have, for the last 15 years, been with principal reference to an entirely new instrument, the Council of Europe Convention on Cybercrime ("Budapest Convention", 2001). The Convention aims to harmonize national cybercrime legislation, enhance transnational policing measures in pursuing and prosecuting cybercriminals, and improve international cybercrime cooperation (Vatis, 2010; Jakobi, 2013: 108–112). The Convention has been signed and ratified by several non-European states, including Canada, Japan, Australia and the United States, and remains open for accession by others. Brazil and India have refused to sign the Convention, as neither played a role in the drafting of the treaty, and Russia claims that transnational policing and investigation violate its sovereignty. China and Russia have suggested that the Shanghai Cooperation Organization is their preferred forum for cybercrime cooperation (Lewis, 2010). Notwithstanding these objections, and issues surrounding its effective implementation (Calderoni, 2010), the Convention is widely regarded as the pre-eminent framework for the prohibition of cybercriminal activities.

The Convention makes no mention of cyberweapons but Article 4.1 requires state parties to criminalize intentional actions in and through computer systems that result in the "damaging, deletion, deterioration, alteration or suppression of computer data without right." Furthermore, state parties may require that such actions "result in serious harm" (Article 4.2). These two articles alone would criminalize the deliberate use of code to cause harm, although the Convention does not further specify to which entities harm must be caused. Article 11 criminalises "aiding and abetting" such activities. There is therefore a range of instances meeting the criteria of intent and harm outlined earlier and the Convention may have further utility in disrupting cyberweapons supply chains. State use of cyberweapons is presumably excepted, although their roles in cyberweapon components markets is legally a grey area and deserves closer attention (Jakobi, 2015; Herzog and Schmid, 2016; Wolf and Fresco, 2016).

The newest source of cyberweapons governance also relies on existing mechanisms, specifically the Wassenaar Arrangement on Export Controls for Conventional Arms and Dual-Use Goods and Technologies (1996). In December 2013, the Arrangement was extended to classes of hardware and software "specially designed or modified for the generation, operation or delivery of, or communication with 'intrusion software,'" defined as software intended to extract or modify data from a computer system or networked device, or which would "allow the execution of externally provided instructions" (Wassenaar Arrangement, 2016). This was the first attempt to incorporate hardware and software associated with cyberweapons into a multilateral regime, although it did not extend to intrusion software itself, into which various cyberweapons components fall. At the end of 2014, EU member-states incorporated the new rules into domestic legislation (Tung, 2014). The United States expressed similar enthusiasm but public consultation revealed significant opposition and in March 2016 the State Department admitted the amendment required renegotiation before translation into domestic law (Barth, 2016). The principal objection was that it would criminalize security researchers using malware systems to improve security products, a potential side-effect recognized since cyberweapons regulation was first discussed (for example, Denning, 2000, 2001). Although "well-intentioned," the amendment would therefore have a negative effect on cybersecurity (Hoffman, 2016).

This indicates clearly the dual-use nature of malware, which can be used for "defensive" and research purposes, as well as "offensive" deployments as cyberweapons proper. In this context, intent determines if malware attains the status of a weapon, not technical considerations (cf. Forge, 2010). It is unclear if the revised Wassenaar Arrangement can be renegotiated to protect legitimate malware uses. Its future efficacy depends on incentivising legitimate security research whilst controlling the export of illegitimate weapons components (Herr, 2016). This task is greatly complicated by Wassenaar's weak enforcement mechanisms, the interplay of state interests, and the technical difficulties in monitoring the transfer of code across the internet (Pyetranker, 2015; Herr, 2016). It does, however, count Russia and the United States as participants, along with 39 other states, which indicates the strength of normative commitments to export controls on dual-use technologies generally.

An emerging global governance architecture

The three fields discussed above—cyberwarfare, cybercrime, export controls—together constitute an emerging global governance architecture for cyberweapons. Each attempts to regulate different aspects of cyberweapons acquisition and use, if not always explicitly in those terms. None is well-advanced institutionally, or in efficacy, as states are still developing cyberweapons and non-state actors still seek to acquire them. Whereas some authors suggest an outright ban on cyberweapons is both possible and desirable (for example, Saran, 2016), the proper frame for considering cyberweapons is regulation, not prohibition. Similarly, whilst ambitions for an overarching treaty framework on cyberweapons are laudable, they founder on well-known obstacles. As Slack (2016: 72) observes of cybersecurity, "the fundamental conception of cyberspace, the lack of a common terminology, the issue of verification, and the dual-use, asymmetric, fast-paced and nonstate-centric nature of the domain … ultimately render a treaty approach unfeasible." Normative approaches are preferred that identify specific issues requiring action, through which "a governance network may emerge where norms of behaviour are developed across a range of fora" (Slack, 2016: 75). One such issue area would be cyberweapons, cooperation over which may be required to settle on "good enough governance" (Grindle, 2004, 2007), rather than aim to close all governance deficits.

This is important because there are significant differences of opinion in all three fields examined here, none of which will be resolved easily but which should not prevent progress being made. Cyberwarfare consensus founders on interpretations of international humanitarian law, particularly as influential *opinio juris* emanates from NATO, to which Russia and China are unsurprisingly resistant. They object similarly to "European" cybercrime initiatives for reasons of sovereignty, which effectively puts two of the world's most important actors outside of the only international convention attempting to regulate cybercrime. The United States objects to the amended Wassenaar Arrangement on the grounds that it undermines security, not that it is seeking to limit its freedom of action, although that dynamic cannot be discounted. The dispute between "the West" and Russia and China, in particular, portends a return to geopolitics in cyberweapons governance, debates over which express deeper concerns about the nature of security in information environments. As rehearsed many times, there is a difference of opinion at the ideological level between broadly liberal nations that prioritize a global, open internet and more authoritarian regimes that seek to regulate the internet along national lines, although liberal states are not exempt from accusations of naked self-interest (Mueller, 2010; DeNardis, 2014; Carr, 2015; Powers and Jablonski, 2015). On the credit side of the ledger, however, there is significantly more cooperation within these fields at present than there has ever been.

Conclusion

This commentary has introduced the concept of cyberweapons governance but is under no illusions that such a discrete policy field currently exists in any formal sense. It does not. It is merely a suggestion that more attention to this issue is required, particularly as practice evolves rapidly and secondary analyses proliferate. As a first step, it has described where cooperation and conflict exist between institutions, norms and major actors, and some of the reasons why. It would also be productive to consider the precise institutional and processual paths by which each of these architectural components has come to exist, as such historical considerations are beyond the scope of this article. The evidence base at present favours analyses of state and intergovernmental initiatives but more research is also required into the actions of civil society, industry and other non-state actors. This would reflect scholarly work on global cybersecurity and internet governance more broadly, which overlaps with some of the concerns raised in this article in both theory and practice (Mueller, 2010; DeNardis, 2014; Nye, 2014; Saran, 2016.

One final suggestion is that fragmentation is inherent to global governance architectures and should not be considered an *a priori* impediment to global cyberweapons governance. This is in contrast to most work on cyberweapons, which presents fragmentation as the antithesis of progress. Instead, fragmentation should be viewed as inevitable and, to a certain extent, as an opportunity. Efforts should be directed towards reducing conflicts over norms and institutions, rather than convergent norms and hierarchical institutions being viewed as prerequisites for effective governance.

Cyberweapons governance is a problematic proposition, on account of environmental complexity; monitoring, verification, compliance and enforcement; and, power politics. The diversity of actors and institutions is also a major challenge but may be its strength. Regulatory innovation emerges not through hierarchies but through diversity. The plethora of public-private partnerships, bilateral agreements, memoranda of understanding, industry initiatives, confidence-building measures and civil society activism, in the broad field of cyber security may encourage the development of novel technical, political and organizational proposals contributing to workable and effective cyberweapons governance. Cyberweapons governance is a daunting prospect but one that needs to be addressed as an emerging security issue. In this respect, fragmentation should be regarded as a condition of progress and as a reaction to the "fuzziness" of the object of governance itself, not as a sign of failure or an excuse for inaction. It took many years to develop effective frameworks for regulating and prohibiting other weapons classes (Mazanec, 2015). None is perfect but each serves the public good better than its absence. So too with cyberweapons. Their full capabilities have yet to be demonstrated but cyberweapons may in future cause substantial harm and damage, maybe even to human life itself. A global governance architecture for cyberweapons is developing quietly and haltingly. It is fragmented and contested but perhaps more constructive than none at all.

References

Arimatsu L (2012) A treaty for governing cyber-weapons: potential benefits and practical limitations. In: Czosseck C, Ottis R and Ziolkowski K (eds). *Proceedings of the 4th International Conference on Cyber Conflict, Tallinn, Estonia, 5–8 June*. CCD COE Publications: Tallinn, pp 91–109.

Barth B (2016) Executive branch concedes Wassenaar Arrangement must be renegotiated, not revised. *SC Magazine* 3 March, http://www

.scmagazine.com/executive-branch-concedes-wassenaar-arrangement
-must-be-renegotiated-not-revised/article/481020/.

Barzashka I (2013) Are cyber-weapons effective? *The RUSI Journal*; 158(2):
48–56.

Biermann F and Pattberg P (2012) Global environmental governance
revisited In: Biermann F and Pattberg P (eds). *Global Environmental
Governance Reconsidered.* The MIT Press: Cambridge, MA, pp 1–23.

Biermann F, Pattberg P, van Asselt H and Zelli F (2009) The fragmentation
of global governance architecture: a framework for analysis. *Global
Environmental Politics*; 9 (4): 14–40.

Boothby B (2016) Cyber weapons: Oxymoron or a real world phenomenon
to be regulated? In: Friis K and Ringsmose J (eds). *Conflict in Cyber
Space: Theoretical, Strategic and Legal Perspectives.* Routledge: Abingdon,
UK; New York, pp 165–174.

Bourne M (2012) Guns don't kill people, cyborgs do: a Latourian
provocation for transformatory arms control and disarmament. *Global
Change, Peace & Security*; 24 (1): 141–163.

Brown D (2006) A proposal for an international convention to regulate the
use of information systems in armed conflict. *Harvard International
Law Journal*; 47 (1): 179–221.

Calderoni F (2010) The European legal framework on cybercrime: striving for
an effective implementation. *Crime, Law & Social Change*; 54(5): 339–357.

Carr M (2015) Power plays in global internet governance. *Millennium:
Journal of International Studies*; 43 (2): 640–659.

Coen D and Pegram T (2015) Wanted: a third generation of global
governance research. *Governance*; 28 (4): 417–420.

Collins S and McCombie S (2012) Stuxnet: the emergence of a new cyber
weapon and its implications. *Journal of Policing, Intelligence & Counter
Terrorism*; 7 (1): 80–91.

Craig A and Valeriano B (2016) Conceptualising cyber arms races. In:
Pissanidis N, Rõigas H and Veenendaal M (eds). *Proceedings of the
8th International Conference on Cyber Conflict: Cyber Power, Tallinn,
Estonia, 31 May-3 June.* CCD COE Publications: Tallinn, pp 141–58.

DeNardis L (2014) *The Global War for Internet Governance.* Yale University
Press: New Haven, CT.

Denning DE (2000) Reflections on cyberweapons controls. *Computer
Security Journal*; 16 (4): 43–53.

Denning DE (2001) Obstacles and options for cyber arms control. Paper
presented at *Arms Control in Cyberspace: Perspectives for Peace Policy in
the Age of Computer Network Attacks* conference, Berlin, 29–30 June.

Dipert RR (2014) The essential features of an ontology for cyberwarfare
In: Yannakogeorgos PA and Lowther AB (eds). *Conflict and Cooperation
in Cyberspace: The Challenge to National Security.* Taylor and Francis:
Boca Raton, FL, pp 35–48.

Eriksson EA (1999) Viewpoint: Information warfare: hype or reality? *The Nonproliferation Review*; 6 (3): 57–64.

Farwell JP and Rohozinski R (2011) Stuxnet and the future of cyber war. *Survival*; 53 (1): 23–40.

Farwell JP and Rohozinski R (2012) The new reality of cyber war. *Survival*; 54 (4): 107–120.

Floridi L (2014) The latent nature of global information warfare. *Philosophy & Technology*; 27 (3): 317–319.

Forge J (2010) A note on the definition of 'dual use'. *Science & Engineering Ethics*; 16 (1): 111–118.

Geers K (2010) Cyber weapons convention. *Computer Law & Security Review*; 26 (5): 547–551.

Grindle MS (2004) Good enough governance: poverty reduction and reform in developing countries. *Governance*; 17 (4): 525–548.

Grindle MS (2007) Good enough governance revisited. *Development Policy Review*; 25 (4): 553–574.

Herr T (2016) Malware counter-proliferation and the Wassenaar Arrangement. In: Pissanidis N, Rõigas H and Veenendaal M (eds). *Proceedings of the 8th International Conference on Cyber Conflict: Cyber Power, Tallinn, Estonia, 31 May-3 June*. CCD COE Publications: Tallinn, pp 175–190.

Herzog M and Schmid J (2016) Who pays for zero-days? Balancing long-term stability in cyber space against short-term national security benefits In: Friis K and Ringsmose J (eds). *Conflict in Cyber Space: Theoretical, Strategic and Legal Perspectives*. Routledge: Abingdon, UK; New York, pp 95–115.

Hofferberth M (2015) Mapping the meanings of global governance: a conceptual reconstruction of a floating signifier. *Millennium: Journal of International Studies*; 43 (2): 598–617.

Hoffman KE (2016) Unsuitable addendum: Wassenaar Arrangement. *SC Magazine* 9 May, https://www.scmagazine.com/unsuitable-addendum -wassenaar-arrangement/article/530284/.

Jakobi AP (2013) Common Goods or Evils? The Formation of Global Crime Governance. Oxford University Press: Oxford.

Jakobi AP (2015) From prohibition to regulation? The global governance of illegal markets. Paper presented at the Comparing the Global Governance of Illegal Markets workshop, October, Bielefeld, Germany.

Krutskikh A and Streltsov A (2014) International law and the problem of international information security. International Affairs [Mezdunarodnaia zhizn]; 60 (6): 64–76.

Lewis JA (2010) Multilateral agreements to constrain cyberconflict. Arms Control Today; 40 (5): 14–19.

Limnéll J (2016) The cyber arms race is accelerating: what are the consequences? Journal of Cyber Policy; 1 (1): 50–60.

Linklater A (2006) The harm principle and global ethics. *Global Society*; 20 (3): 329–343.

Maybaum M and Tölle J (2016) Arms control in cyberspace: architecture for a trust-based implementation framework based on conventional arms control methods. In: Pissanidis N, Rõigas H and Veenendaal M (eds). *Proceedings of the 8th International Conference on Cyber Conflict: Cyber Power, Tallinn, Estonia, 31 May-3 June.* CCD COE Publications: Tallinn, pp 159–173.

Mazanec BM (2015) *The Evolution of Cyber War: International Norms for Emerging-Technology Weapons.* Potomac Books: Lincoln, NE.

Mele S (2013) *Cyber-Weapons: Legal and Strategic Aspects*; version 2.0, June Italian Institute of Strategic Studies: Rome, Italy.

Meyer P (2011) Cyber-security through arms control: an approach to international co-operation. *The RUSI Journal*; 156 (2): 22–27.

Ministry of Defence. (2013) *Cyber Primer.* Ministry of Defence: London.

Mueller ML (2010) *Networks and States: The Global Politics of Internet Governance.* The MIT Press: Cambridge, MA.

NATO. (2014) Wales Summit Declaration. Press release, 5 September, http://www.nato.int/cps/en/natohq/official_texts_112964.htm.

NATO Cooperative Cyber Defence Centre of Excellence (CCD COE). (2015) Tallinn Manual 2.0 to be completed in 2016. Press release, 9 October, https://ccdcoe.org/tallinn-manual-20-be-completed-2016.html.

Nye JS Jr (2014) *The Regime Complex for Managing Global Cyber Activities.* Global Commission on Internet Governance Paper Series 1. Global Commission on Internet Governance: Waterloo, ON and Chatham House: London.

Powers SM and Jablonski M (2015) *The Real Cyber War: The Political Economy of Internet Freedom.* University of Illinois Press: Urbana, Chicago and Springfield, IL.

Prunckun H (2008) 'Bogies in the wire': Is there a need for legislative control of cyber weapons? *Global Crime*; 9 (3): 262–272.

Pyetranker I (2015) An umbrella in a hurricane: Cyber technology and the December 2013 amendment to the wassenaar arrangement. *Northwestern Journal of Technology & Intellectual Property*; 13 (2): 153–180.

Rathmell A (2003) Controlling computer network operations. *Studies in Conflict & Terrorism*; 26 (3): 215–232.

Rid T (2013) *Cyber War Will Not Take Place.* Hurst & Company: London.

Rid T and McBurney P (2012) Cyber-weapons. *The RUSI Journal*; 157 (1): 6–13.

Sanger DE (2012) *Confront and Conceal: Obama's Secret Wars and Surprising Use of American Power.* Crown Publishers: New York.

Saran S (2016) Striving for an international consensus on cyber security: lessons from the 20th century. *Global Policy*; 7 (1): 93–95.

Schmitt MN (ed) (2013) *Tallinn Manual on the International Law Applicable to Cyber Warfare.* Cambridge University Press: Cambridge, UK.

Singer PW and Friedman A (2014) *Cybersecurity and Cyberwar: What Everyone Needs to Know*. Oxford University Press: New York.

Slack C (2016) Wired yet disconnected: the governance of international cyber relations. *Global Policy*; 7 (1): 69–78.

Sofaer AD and Goodman SE (2000) *A Proposal for an International Convention on Cyber Crime and Terrorism*. Working paper. Stanford University: Stanford, CA.

Stevens T (2016a) *Cyber Security and the Politics of Time*. Cambridge University Press: Cambridge, UK.

Stevens T (2016b) Cyberweapons: governing the ungovernable? *Political Studies Association* blog, 28 June, https://www.psa.ac.uk/insight-plus/blog/cyberweapons-governing-ungovernable.

Tung L (2014) EU exploit vendors will need a 'licence to sell' from 31 December. *CSO Online*, 19 December, http://www.cso.com.au/article/562845/eu-exploit-vendors-will-need-licence-sell-from-31-december.

US Department of Defense. (2015a) *Cyber Strategy*. Department of Defense: Washington DC.

US Department of Defense. (2015b) *Law of War Manual*. Office of General Counsel, Department of Defense: Washington DC.

Valeriano B, Roff H and Lawson S (2016) Dropping the cyber bomb? Spectacular claims and unremarkable effects. *Council on Foreign Relations* blog, 24 May, http://blogs.cfr.org/cyber/2016/05/24/dropping-the-cyber-bomb-spectacular-claims-and-unremarkable-effects.

Vatis MA (2010) The Council of Europe Convention on Cybercrime. In: *Proceedings of a Workshop on Deterring CyberAttacks: Informing Strategies and Developing Options for US Policy, 10–11 June, Washington, DC*. The National Academies Press: Washington DC, pp 207–223.

von Heinegg WH (2015) *International Law and International Information Security: A Response to Krutskikh and Streltsov*. Tallinn Paper no. 9. CCD COE Publications: Tallinn.

Wassenaar Arrangement. (2016) *List of Dual-Use Goods and Technologies and Munitions List*. WA-LIST (15) 1 Corr. 1, 4 April, http://www.wassenaar.org/wp-content/uploads/2016/04/WA-LIST-15-1-CORR-1-2015-List-of-DU-Goods-and-Technologies-and-Munitions-List.pdf..

Wolf MJ and Fresco N (2016) Ethics of the software vulnerabilities and exploits market. *The Information Society: An International Journal*; 32(4): 269–279.

Zetter K (2014) *Countdown to Zero Day: Stuxnet and the Launch of the World's First Digital Weapon*. Crown Publishers: New York.

Zumbansen P (2012) Governance: an interdisciplinary perspective In: Levi-Faur D (ed). *The Oxford Handbook of Governance*. Oxford University Press: Oxford, pp 83–96.

11

Accountability for Cyberattacks Is Difficult

Siraj Ahmed Shaikh

Siraj Ahmed Shaikh is a professor of systems security at Coventry University in the UK and the founder and CSO of CyberOwl, a systems security software company. His main research interest lies in systems security, essentially at the intersection of cybersecurity, systems engineering and traditional computer science.

Holding particular individuals accountable for a cyberattack is not an easy task. Government, the immense preparation behind an attack, and internet traffic all play a role in making it difficult to place blame. In the following article from 2014, Siraj Ahmed Shaikh breaks down some of the challenges and points out, "Cyber-attacks can be launched with relatively little software, hardware and skills, but can have an enormous impact in terms of cost and disruption."

Who's in your network, checking out your data? The latest invasive digital creature is Sandworm, a piece of malware discovered to be using a previously unknown Windows vulnerability to infiltrate government networks, spying on systems at NATO, the European Union, the Ukrainian government and others.

In recent years a number of such attacks have been about espionage: stealing sensitive information, or disrupting the critical infrastructure that nations depend on. Making use of sophisticated techniques and zero-day exploits (security vulnerabilities that have not been publicly announced), they are the result of considerable skills and resources.

With targets more political than commercial or criminal in nature, the suspicion is that, due to their deliberate and persistent pursuit of goals aligned with national interests, the attacks have state sponsors.

This is a worrying trend. Cyberattacks can be launched with relatively little software, hardware and skills, but can have an enormous impact in terms of cost and disruption. As global networks grow in terms of traffic, speed and reach, the situation is only going to get worse.

One serious problem is the difficulty in attributing with any confidence a particular attack to its nation of origin. The internet's technical architecture was built to provide open connectivity, not accountability.

This is complicated by how multistage attacks, which most modern cyberattacks are, make it near impossible to assert any reliable attribution. These operations are set up so that the attacker first compromises a third party's computer in order to use it as a proxy platform to launch an attack on the final target.

There may be several such machines, each used to compromise another, creating a complex web of connections that obscure the attack's origin. This chain can be sustained in order to allow data to be extracted from the target and brought back, undercover, to the attacker.

Pointing the finger

Some nations including Russia, China, and Israel are thought to maintain cyberwarfare teams and carry out state-sponsored attacks. For example, the security research firm Mandiant recently identified a suspected Chinese military cyberwarfare team, Unit 61398, down to the location of its building. This led the US government to file criminal charges for hacking against five named Chinese military officers.

Attributing cyberattacks follows the principle of sophistication, examining the level of skills and resources required to pull off the attack. The use of zero-day exploits, for example, demonstrates considerable time and effort has gone into testing for an unknown vulnerability against which the target will have little protection. This is not likely to be something a bedroom hacker could achieve.

Attacks that are persistent, trying to overcome defences rather than looking elsewhere for easier targets, are also a sign of possible state backing. This is especially when the target is to steal sensitive information—such as the details of the US F-35 stealth fighter apparently lost to Chinese cyberespionage—rather than just financial gain.

In the case of Sandworm the context of the conflict in Ukraine is a further giveaway, judging by the military and political organisations targeted and the intelligence-related documents sought.

Signals in the noise

The characteristics of internet traffic make its attribution more difficult still. The rising volume of non-productive traffic, such as network scanning, worms, traffic resulting from misconfigured routers or systems, and web indexing crawlers such as Googlebot, creates background noise.

The problem is that this background noise may also resemble genuine malicious attacks – in fact, it's difficult to determine what is accidental and what is deliberate. This leaves a great number of false positives recorded in firewall logs which only makes pinpointing genuine attacks harder.

At the political level, any accusation of state-sponsored hacking needs to be backed up with proof. More often than not, however, the proxy launch pads for most multistage attacks are based in non-hostile states. The *Tallinn Manual*, the most comprehensive legal cyberwarfare rulebook, states that those on the receiving end of any cyberattack can only respond by applying the "unwilling or unable" test. This is an underlying principle of international law which asserts that retaliation against an intermediary state used by an enemy to launch an attack is only permissible if the intermediary is either unwilling or unable to prevent the aggressor responsible from doing so.

Perhaps the greatest difficulty posed by any retaliatory cyberattack is the geopolitics of the day. Political alliances, intelligence sharing, legal and ethical considerations, and potential sensitivity of offensive operations, all make it very difficult for nation states to launch such operations. The result is that the sort of public accusations of cyberattacks seen in the press and meant as a tool of deterrence are almost entirely useless—as can be seen Russia and China's frequent and easy denials.

12

Can Political Strategy Be Applied to Cyberspace?

Joseph S. Nye

Political scientist Joseph S. Nye is a former US assistant secretary of defense for international security affairs and one-time chairman of the National Intelligence Council. Now commissioner for the Global Commission on Internet Governance, he is also the author of books like Soft Power: The Means to Success in World Politics *and* Is the American Century Over?

The creation of a cyberspace treaty would be politically possible, but that does not mean other methods can't be applied. One way to succeed is to look not at the weapons involved, but rather the target of an attack. In the following piece from the spring of 2017, Joseph Nye looks at the troubling history of conflicts in both cyberspace and the physical world and questions how to contain the threats posed by all kinds of weapons.

A series of episodes in recent years—including Russia's cyberinterventions to skew the United States' 2016 presidential election toward Donald Trump, the anonymous cyberattacks that disrupted Ukraine's electricity system in 2015, and the "Stuxnet" virus that destroyed a thousand Iranian centrifuges—has fueled growing concern about conflict in cyberspace. At last month's Munich Security Conference, Dutch Foreign Minister Bert

"A Normative Approach to Preventing Cyberwarfare," by Joseph S. Nye, Project Syndicate, March 13, 2017. Reprinted by Permission.

Koenders announced the formation of a new non-governmental Global Commission on the Stability of Cyberspace to supplement the UN Group of Governmental Experts (GGE).

The GGE's reports in 2010, 2013, and 2015 helped to set the negotiating agenda for cybersecurity, and the most recent identified a set of norms that have been endorsed by the UN General Assembly. But, despite this initial success, the GGE has limitations. The participants are technically advisers to the UN Secretary-General rather than fully empowered national negotiators. Although the number of participants has increased from the original 15 to 25, most countries do not have a voice.

But there is a larger question lurking behind the GGE: Can norms really limit state behavior?

Most experts agree that a global cyberspace treaty currently would be politically impossible (though Russia and China have made such proposals at the UN). But, beyond formal treaties, normative constraints on states also include codes of conduct, conventional state practices, and widely shared expectations of proper behavior among a group (which create a common law). In scope, these constraints can vary from global, to plurilateral, to bilateral. So what can history tell us about the effectiveness of normative policy instruments?

In the decade after Hiroshima, tactical nuclear weapons were widely regarded as "normal" weapons, and the US military incorporated nuclear artillery, atomic land mines, and nuclear anti-aircraft weapons into its deployed forces. In 1954 and 1955, the Chairman of the Joint Chiefs of Staff told President Dwight Eisenhower that the defense of Dien Bien Phu in Vietnam and of offshore islands near Taiwan would require the use of nuclear weapons (Eisenhower rejected the advice).

Over time, the development of an informal norm of non-use of nuclear weapons changed this. The Nobel laureate economist Thomas Schelling argued that the development of the norm of non-use of nuclear weapons was one of the most important aspects of arms control over the past 70 years, and it has had an inhibiting effect on decision-makers. But for new nuclear states like North Korea, one cannot be sure that the costs of violating the taboo would be perceived as outweighing the benefits.

Similarly, a taboo against using poisonous gases in warfare developed after World War I, and the 1925 Geneva Protocol prohibited the use of chemical and biological weapons. Two treaties in the 1970s prohibited the production and stockpiling of such weapons, creating a cost not only for their use, but also for their very possession.

Verification provisions for the Biological Weapons Convention are weak (merely reporting to the UN Security Council), and such taboos did not prevent the Soviet Union from continuing to possess and develop biological weapons in the 1970s. Similarly, the Chemical Weapons Convention did not stop either Saddam Hussein or Bashar al-Assad from using chemical weapons against their own citizens.

Nonetheless, both treaties have shaped how others perceive such actions. Such perceptions contributed to the justification of the invasion of Iraq in 2003 and to the international dismantling of most Syrian weapons in 2014. With 173 countries having ratified the Biological Warfare Convention, states that wish to develop such weapons must do so secretly, and face widespread international condemnation if evidence of their activities becomes known.

Normative taboos may also become relevant in the cyber realm, though here the difference between a weapon and a non-weapon depends on intent, and it would be difficult to forbid – and impossible to prohibit reliably – the design, possession, or even implantation for espionage of particular computer programs. In that sense, efforts to prevent cyber conflict cannot be like the nuclear arms control that developed during the Cold War, which involved elaborate treaties and detailed verification protocols.

A more fruitful approach to normative controls on cyberwarfare may be to establish a taboo not against *weapons* but against *targets*. The US has promoted the view that the Law of Armed Conflict (LOAC), which prohibit deliberate attacks on civilians, applies in cyberspace. Accordingly, the US has proposed that, rather than pledging "no first use" of cyberweapons, countries should pledge not to use cyberweapons against civilian facilities in peacetime.

This approach to norms has been adopted by the GGE. The taboo would be reinforced by confidence-building measures such as promises of forensic assistance and noninterference with the workings of Computer Security Incident Response Teams (CSIRTs).

The GGE report of July 2015 focused on restraining attacks on certain civilian targets, rather than proscribing particular code. At the September 2015 summit between US President Barack Obama and Chinese President Xi Jinping, the two leaders agreed to establish an expert commission to study the GGE proposal. Subsequently, the GGE report was endorsed by the leaders of the G20 and referred to the UN General Assembly.

The attack on the Ukrainian power system occurred in December 2015, shortly after the submission of the GGE report, and in 2016, Russia did not treat the US election process as protected civilian infrastructure. The development of normative controls on cyberweapons remains a slow—and, at this point, incomplete—process.

13

Cyberwarfare Is Like the Wild West

Shahrooz Shekaraubi

Shahrooz Shekaraubi, one of the very first students to earn a bachelor's degree in Persian Studies from the Roshan Center of Persian Studies at the University of Maryland, is now the founder and president of the Aftab Committee.

The United States and Iran have given a glimpse into what future wars will look like—proving that cyberattacks can cause serious harm—and, yet, lawmakers are still unwilling to consider cyberattacks as a real threat instead of something thought of by television and movies. In the following piece, Shahrooz Shekaraubi stresses the need for clear definitions of what cyberwarfare entails and cautions governments and international organizations against treating cybercrime like they would treat any other conflict.

During a recent speech to university students, Iran's Supreme Leader Ayatollah Khamenei urged the country's students to prepare for cyberwar, the semi-official Mehr News Agency reported last Wednesday. Calling the students "cyberwar agents" he reminded them of their special role in this particular kind of war and that Tehran is prepared for a cyber battle against the United States and Israel.

Ayatollah Khamenei's remarks are believed to be a response to Israel's Major General Aviv Kochavi, who went on record as

"The Wild West of Cyberwarfare," by Shahrooz Shekaraubi, *International Policy Digest*, February 26, 2014. Reprinted by Permission.

saying, "cyber, in my modest opinion, will soon be revealed to be the biggest revolution in warfare, more than gunpowder and the utilization of air power in the last century." These remarks are a powerful reminder of the uncertainty of future international cyberwarfare and how unregulated it is.

Over the past decade, the United States and Iran have changed the definition of traditional warfare giving the international community a glimpse into what future wars will look like. In the past decade, both countries have extensively built up their cyber arsenals launching sophisticated assaults on each other's computer networks, banks and sensitive infrastructure. It could be argued that the United States has been more successful but Iran is catching up. It is clear that when these cyberattacks do grow in escalation they may potentially have a serious humanitarian impact. Yet, international law has not been absent in addressing the cyberwar domain. For many, cyberwar and cybersecurity is seen as still the 'stuff' you see in summer blockbusters and not for what it really is: serious, perplexing and scary.

Michael Schmitt, a professor at the U.S. Naval War College, when asked in an interview with the CBC what international laws governs cyberwarfare, "The answer is there's nothing and there's everything."

However, he stressed, "If you're looking for cyber specific law, a law that says 'a cyberattack that causes these consequences in an armed attack to which you can respond,' you will find nothing," he said. "But it was our unanimous consensus among the group of experts that the existing international law applies to cyberspace and to cyberweapons."

This has left the international community vulnerable to a kind of cyber wild west. Since everything is interconnected – the key challenge is to ensure that any cyberattacks are directed against military objectives and that ordinary civilians along with civilian infrastructure is protected. Governments have an important responsibility in being extremely cautious in cyberwarfare. But why hasn't the international community implemented official legal structures on the conduct or justification of cyberwarfare? And what can world citizens do to deter the threat of cyberwarfare?

Clear definitions

One of the main challenges in international cybersecurity is that there is still not a widely agreed upon set of definitions on what cyberwarfare and its related dimensions are. Defining the terms and dimensions of cyberwarfare, such as cybercrime, cyberterrorism, and cyberattacks is important in deterring cyberthreats. Until recently there have been two major state-led efforts to define the scope and range of cyberwarfare, one by the United States and the other by the Shanghai Cooperation Organization. Unsurprisingly, not only do their understandings and definitions differ but they both have tremendous ambiguity, overlap and coverage gaps.

While the US government mostly takes on an objective-based definition of cyberthreats, the Shanghai Cooperation Organization, on the other hand, adopts a more expansive means based definition of cyberwarfare to include the dissemination of information to undermine political, economic and spiritual stability in a country. The gap between these two major government-led understandings of cyberwarfare only adds to the threat and our global cyber-insecurity. Before cyberattacks escalate between countries or groups, world citizens must organize and urge their governments to sit down and specifically define the range and scope of cyberwarfare. This is vital as it will be these clear definitions and understanding that will guide how international law on cyberwarfare will proscribe its range and scope and justification by a state.

International law and cyberwarfare

The ambiguities of cyberwarfare are worrisome for ordinary people and governments alike. The existing law of war structure and framework- that includes, *jus ad bellum* and *jus in bella*, provides some limited guidelines for states seeking an answer to cyberwarfare. Some military experts reaffirm the law of war as a proper body of laws to address this issue. However, this code of laws fails to cover the entire range and scope of cyberwarfare activities.

International legal frameworks such as the United Nations, Council of Europe, NATO, Organization of American States and the Shanghai Cooperation Organization have all provided inadequate efforts on definitions and legal structures.

All these international bodies have shown growing interest in cybersecurity and addressing issues pertaining to cyberwarfare. Yet they have failed in establishing an effective legal framework that can govern all cyberattacks. Once clear definitions are made, dialogue between states can lead to international cooperation on ratifying rigorous international laws and legal structures that can serve as a limit on cyber warfare.

Cyberwarfare and world safety

The first effort to combat this insecurity is to have the Geneva and Hague conventions apply clear principles related to cyber warfare. These principles and agreements on cyberwarfare, for example, must designate sensitive infrastructure such as nuclear energy plants, hospitals and electronic records such as university or medical records as red lines. Moreover, although international norms on cyberwarfare would be effective, the international community must also understand that any international laws implemented on cyberwarfare must be interpreted only in a cybercontext. States and international organizations must avoid merely interpreting the nature of the threat of cyberwarfare. Rather, the severity of the consequences of cyberattacks that can result in the loss of thousands of innocent lives and severe damage to civilian infrastructure must be emphasized.

We are in the early years of cyberwarfare and the US-Iran cyberwar is just one of many wars to come. It's scary. It's destabilizing. It's no summer blockbuster and the threat can destroy the fabric of our world. Besides clarifying definitions and implementing international cyber laws, our only remaining choice is to urge our governments to sign cyberwar peace treaties. This won't magically make this threat go away, but it will make our world safer.

14

Should National Security and Cybersecurity Go Hand in Hand?

Stuart Madnick

Stuart Madnick is the John Norris Maguire professor of information technology, a professor of information technology and engineering systems, and the codirector of the PROFIT Program at the MIT Sloan School of Management. Madnick, who also has a PhD in computer science from MIT, finds ways to integrate information systems to provide organizations with a more global view of their operations.

The National Security Agency was the victim of a cyberattack in 2016, leading many to wonder just how "secure" the agency—and the US government—really is. In the following article, Stuart Madnick explores whether a partnership between the NSA and the military's Cyber Command is the best way to combat future threats. "We do not want to wait until World War Cyber is upon us to resolve the debate this time," warns Madnick. "We need to have a fully functional fighting force capable of taking offensive action in the case of potential, and likely, cyberwarfare."

The National Security Agency is the nation's digital spying organization. U.S. Cyber Command is a military unit focused on cyberwarfare. Does it make sense for one person to lead them both at the same time?

"Should NSA and Cyber Command have separate leadership?" by Stuart Madnick, *The Conversation*, October 5, 2016. https://theconversation.com/should-nsa-and-cyber-command-have-separate-leadership-65986. CC BY-ND 4.0

That has been the case since Cyber Command's inception in 2009. But recently, Defense Secretary Ashton Carter and Director of National Intelligence James Clapper have been urging President Obama to divide the two leadership roles. The change, they say, would help Cyber Command become an independent fighting force that doesn't require support from another agency—the NSA.

The NSA's job is a defensive one, monitoring internet communications worldwide and gathering information to help the government understand what other countries are doing (or planning), and to resist foreign efforts to learn about what the U.S. is up to. By contrast, Cyber Command is a military unit, with a largely offensive mission. It is tasked with ensuring that the U.S. has unchallenged online superiority, able to shut down or disrupt the cyberoperations and networks of adversaries.

Clearly there are similarities that suggest the two agencies should cooperate and share knowledge. For example, the NSA needs to penetrate foreign networks to collect data. Cyber Command also needs to break into others' computer systems, though for a very different purpose, such as shutting down an electric power grid. As a scholar of both information technology and management, I know that the key factor to consider in deciding on joint or separate leadership is not cooperation, but rather focus.

Given their respective offensive and defensive roles, separate leadership would be the best way to provide clear direction for each.

Sharing leadership

There are precedents for sharing—and splitting—leadership. There is, of course, the current situation, in which the NSA and Cyber Command are both headed by Navy Admiral Michael S. Rogers. In the military, this is often called a "dual-hat arrangement," because one leader "wears two hats" by holding two posts at the same time.

A useful example from history is the evolution of the U.S. Army Air Corps. From its formation in 1926 to 1941, the Army Air Corps was primarily used to support ground troops, rather than as an offensive force in its own right. During that period, though, there was continuous debate about whether air and ground units would work better with separate leadership.

As World War II began and strategists' understanding of the strength of airborne weapons developed, the groundwork was laid for separating ground and air power: In a 1941 administrative reorganization of the Army, the renamed Army Air Force became one of three independent commands. In 1947 the split was complete with the creation of the U.S. Air Force that we know today.

We do not want to wait until World War Cyber is upon us to resolve the debate this time. We need to have a fully functional fighting force capable of taking offensive action in the case of potential, and likely, cyberwarfare.

Overlapping technology

Both the NSA and Cyber Command use computers and computer networks. Both use—and seek to break—encryption software as well as tools to hack into networks, such as phishing methods, and various types of malware to extract information.

In the military there are plenty of examples of different units relying on similar tools. For instance, look at aircraft use. In addition to the Air Force, the Army, Navy, Marines and Coast Guard all use planes and helicopters. Some of those aircraft are even identical (or nearly so), such as the C-130 "Hercules" cargo plane and the UH-60 "Black Hawk" helicopter. Just because different groups use the same equipment does not mean they must share a single leader.

Determining relative priority

We can also take a lesson from the corporate world, where responsibilities vary widely. In a panel discussion that I led in May, questions to the audience revealed that in some companies, the head of cybersecurity defense efforts reports to the head of the information technology department. But in other cases the cybersecurity chief reported to the chief financial officer, or even to the head of the company's legal department. Increasingly we are hearing that cybersecurity leaders report directly to the firm's CEO.

The panel members viewed cybersecurity as an inherently cautious task, where evaluating risk is important. By contrast, information technology departments often push for rapid innovation and accelerating change. As a result of those conflicting goals, the panelists came to the consensus that those efforts should be managed separately.

Using similar logic, I believe that the NSA and Cyber Command should be under separate leadership, so each can pursue its mission with undivided focus and complete intensity. The NSA can gather intelligence. Cyber Command can defend our military networks and be ready to attack the systems of our enemies.

15

Cyberdeterrence Is the Next Step in Cybersecurity

Dorothy Denning

Dorothy E. Denning is emeritus distinguished professor of defense analysis at the Naval Postgraduate School. Her teaching and research focuses on cybersecurity and cyberconflict. She has testified before the US Congress on encryption policy and cyberterrorism and was inducted into the inaugural class of the National Cyber Security Hall of Fame. Denning is also the author of Information Warfare and Security.

More and more wars are being fought on cyberbattlefields, and the tried-and-true methods of combating hackers are having little impact. In the following piece, Dorothy Denning suggests treating cyberwarfare just like the US government treats regular warfare— with the two principles of deterrence: denial and punishment. "For decades, deterrence has effectively countered the threat of nuclear weapons. Can we achieve similar results against cyberweapons?" she asks, before offering three measures for implementing cyberdeterrence.

Cyberattackers pose many threats to a wide range of targets. Russia, for example, was accused of hacking Democratic Party computers throughout the year, interfering with the U.S. presidential election. Then there was the unknown attacker who,

"Cybersecurity's next phase: Cyber-deterrence," by Dorothy Denning, *The Conversation*, December 12, 2016. https://theconversation.com/cybersecuritys-next-phase-cyber -deterrence-67090. CC BY-ND 4.0

on a single October day, used thousands of internet-connected devices, such as digital video recorders and cameras compromised by Mirai malware, to take down several high-profile websites, including Twitter.

From 2005 to 2015, federal agencies reported a 1,300 percent jump in cybersecurity incidents. Clearly, we need better ways of addressing this broad category of threats. Some of us in the cybersecurity field are asking whether cyber deterrence might help.

Deterrence focuses on making potential adversaries think twice about attacking, forcing them to consider the costs of doing so, as well as the consequences that might come from a counterattack. There are two main principles of deterrence. The first, denial, involves convincing would-be attackers that they won't succeed, at least without enormous effort and cost beyond what they are willing to invest. The second is punishment: Making sure the adversaries know there will be a strong response that might inflict more harm than they are willing to bear.

For decades, deterrence has effectively countered the threat of nuclear weapons. Can we achieve similar results against cyberweapons?

Why cyberdeterrence is hard

Nuclear deterrence works because few countries have nuclear weapons or the significant resources needed to invest in them. Those that do have them recognize that launching a first strike risks a devastating nuclear response. Further, the international community has established institutions, such as the International Atomic Energy Agency, and agreements, such as the Treaty on the Non-Proliferation of Nuclear Weapons, to counter the catastrophic threat nuclear weapons pose.

Cyberweapons are nothing like nuclear ones. They are readily developed and deployed by individuals and small groups as well as states. They are easily replicated and distributed across networks, rendering impossible the hope of anything that might be called "cyber nonproliferation." Cyberweapons are often deployed under a cloak of anonymity, making it difficult to figure out who is really responsible. And cyberattacks can achieve a broad range of effects, most of which are disruptive and costly, but not catastrophic.

This does not mean cyberdeterrence is doomed to failure. The sheer scale of cyberattacks demands that we do better to defend against them.

There are three things we can do to strengthen cyberdeterrence: Improve cybersecurity, employ active defenses and establish international norms for cyberspace. The first two of these measures will significantly improve our cyberdefenses so that even if an attack is not deterred, it will not succeed.

Stepping up protection

Cybersecurity aids deterrence primarily through the principle of denial. It stops attacks before they can achieve their goals. This includes beefing up login security, encrypting data and communications, fighting viruses and other malware, and keeping software updated to patch weaknesses when they're found.

But even more important is developing products that have few if any security vulnerabilities when they are shipped and installed. The Mirai botnet, capable of generating massive data floods that overload internet servers, takes over devices that have gaping security holes, including default passwords hardcoded into firmware that users can't change. While some companies such as Microsoft invest heavily in product security, others, including many Internet-of-Things vendors, do not.

Cybersecurity guru Bruce Schneier aptly characterizes the prevalence of insecure Internet-of-Things devices as a market failure akin to pollution. Simply put, the market favors cheap insecure devices over ones that are more costly but secure. His solution? Regulation, either by imposing basic security standards on manufacturers, or by holding them liable when their products are used in attacks.

Active defenses

When it comes to taking action against attackers, there are many ways to monitor, identify and counter adversary cyberattacks. These active cyberdefenses are similar to air defense systems that monitor the sky for hostile aircraft and shoot down incoming missiles. Network monitors that watch for and block ("shoot down") hostile packets are one example, as are honeypots that attract or deflect adversary packets into safe areas. There, they do not harm the targeted network, and can even be studied to reveal attackers' techniques.

Another set of active defenses involves collecting, analyzing and sharing information about potential threats so that network operators can respond to the latest developments. For example, operators could regularly scan their systems looking for devices vulnerable to or compromised by the Mirai botnet or other malware. If they found some, they could disconnect the devices from the network and alert the devices' owners to the danger.

Active cyberdefense does more than just deny attackers opportunities. It can often unmask the people behind them, leading to punishment. Nongovernment attackers can be shut down, arrested and prosecuted; countries conducting or supporting cyberwarfare can be sanctioned by the international community.

Currently, however, the private sector is reluctant to employ many active defenses because of legal uncertainties. The Center for Cyber and Homeland Security at George Washington University recommends several actions that the government and the private sector could take to enable more widespread use of active defenses, including clarifying regulations.

Setting international norms

Finally, international norms for cyberspace can aid deterrence if national governments believe they would be named and shamed within the international community for conducting a cyberattack. The U.S. brought charges in 2014 against five Chinese military hackers for targeting American companies. A year later, the U.S.

and China agreed to not steal and exploit each other's corporate secrets for commercial advantage. In the wake of those events, cyberespionage from China plummeted.

Also in 2015, a U.N. group of experts recommended banning cyberattacks against critical infrastructure, including a country's computer emergency response teams. And later that year, the G20 issued a statement opposing the theft of intellectual property to benefit commercial entities. These norms might deter governments from conducting such attacks.

Cyberspace will never be immune to attack—no more than our streets will be immune to crime. But with stronger cybersecurity, increased use of active cyberdefenses, and international cybernorms, we can hope to at least keep a lid on the problem.

Organizations to Contact

The editors have compiled the following list of organizations concerned with the issues debated in this book. The descriptions are derived from materials provided by the organizations. All have publications or information available for interested readers. The list was compiled on the date of publication of the present volume; the information provided here may change. Be aware that many organizations take several weeks or longer to respond to inquiries, so allow as much time as possible.

CCDCOE
Filtri tee 12
Tallinn 10132, Estonia
phone: +372 7176 800
email: ccdcoe@ccdcoe.org
website: www.ccdcoe.org

The NATO Cooperative Cyber Defense Centre of Excellence (CCDCOE) supports the members of NATO with cyberdefense expertise in technology, strategy, operations, and law. As of 2017, Belgium, the Czech Republic, Estonia, France, Germany, Greece, Hungary, Italy, Latvia, Lithuania, the Netherlands, Poland, Slovakia, Spain, Turkey, the United Kingdom, and the United States are signed on as sponsoring nations. Austria and Finland have become contributing participants and Sweden is on its way to doing the same. The centre is staffed and financed by member nations and is not part of NATO's military command or force structure.

Center for Internet Security (CIS)
31 Tech Valley Drive
East Greenbush, NY 12061
phone: 518-266-3460

email: contact@cisecurity.org
website: www.cisecurity.org

The Center for Internet Security uses a team of IT professionals to protect both public and private organizations from cyberthreats. Their CIS Controls and CIS Benchmarks are a global standard for securing IT systems and data against the most pervasive attacks. Their mission is to identify, develop, validate, promote, and sustain best practice solutions for cyberdefense while also building and leading communities to enable an environment of trust in cyberspace.

(ISC)²

311 Park Place Boulevard
Suite 400
Clearwater, FL 33759
phone: 727-785-0189
email: communications@isc2.org
website: www.isc2.org

(ISC)² is a nonprofit membership organization that focuses on promoting a safe and secure cyberworld and empowering information security leaders. Founded in 1989, the organization is composed of more than 125,000 information, software, and infrastructure security professionals who help advance the technological industry.

LIFARS

244 Fifth Avenue
Suite 2305
New York, NY 10001
phone: 212-222-7061
email: contact@lifars.com
website: www.lifars.com

Liberty Investigation Forensic and Response Services (LIFARS) is a global cybersecurity intelligence firm based in New York. LIFARS helps businesses defend their networks and reputation by providing elite cybersecurity solutions in incident response, digital forensics and cybersecurity intelligence. They also conduct digital forensic investigations, data breach incident response, web application security testing, and digital risk assessments.

National Cyber Security Alliance
website: www.staysafeonline.org

The goal of the National Cyber Security Alliance, which works with the US Department of Homeland Security, is to educate and empower everyone to use the internet securely and safety. A nonprofit founded in 2001, they provide a variety of programs for individuals as well as government, industry, nonprofit and academic sectors.

National Cybersecurity Student Association
301 Largo Rd, Rm 129C
Largo, Maryland 20774
phone: 785-813-1202
email: info@cyberstudents.org
website: www.cyberstudents.org

The National Cybersecurity Student Association supports cybersecurity programs in academic institutions across the United States. They work through networking, activities, and collaboration and serve as a one-stop-shop to enhance the educational and professional development of cybersecurity students.

OWASP (Open Web Application Security Project)
1200-C Agora Drive, #232
Bel Air, MD 21014
phone: 951-692-7703
fax: 443-283-4021
email: owasp.foundation@owasp.org
website: www.owasp.org

The Open Web Application Security Project (OWASP) is a nonprofit organization dedicated to making software more secure.

A global group of volunteers with more than forty-five thousand participants, they strive to provide information to individuals and companies so that they may make well-rounded decisions about technology and safety.

RAND Corporation
PO Box 2138
1776 Main Street
Santa Monica, CA 90407
phone: 310-393-0411
website: www.rand.org

The RAND Corporation is a nonprofit, nonpartisan research organization that addresses issues around the world pertaining to sustainability, development, health, and security. Established in 1948, RAND brings together the finest researchers in the world and utilizes the very best analytical tools and methods to develop objective policy solutions. They deliver fact-based, actionable solutions grounded in rigorous analysis.

SANS Institute
8120 Woodmont Avenue, Suite 310
Bethesda, MD 20814
phone: 301-654-7267
fax: (301) 951-0140
email: info@sans.org
website: www.sans.org

The SANS Institute claims to be the largest source for information security training and security certification in the world. It holds the most information about internet security and operates the internet's early warning system, the Internet Storm Center. Established in 1989 as a cooperative research and education organization, its goal is to facilitate prevention of, and defense against, cyberthreats.

US-CERT

Mailstop: 0635
245 Murray Lane SW Bldg 410
Washington, DC 20528
phone: 888-282-0870
email: soc@us-cert.gov
website: www.us-cert.gov

The United States Computer Emergency Readiness Team (US-CERT) providing cybersecurity protection to federal civilian executive branch agencies through intrusion detection and prevention capabilities and responds to all major incidents—analyzing threats and exchanging critical cybersecurity information with trusted partners around the world. They were formed in early 2000 in response to a high number of cyberbreaches.

Bibliography

Books

Bobby Akart. *Cyber Warfare: Prepping for Tomorrow*. Freedom Preppers, Inc., 2015. Print.

Julia Angwin. *Dragnet Nation: A Quest for Privacy, Security, and Freedom in a World of Relentless Surveillance*. New York, NY: St. Martin's Griffin, 2015.

Jeffrey Carr. *Inside Cyber Warfare: Mapping the Cyber Underworld*. Sebastopol, CA: O'Reilly Media, 2012.

Richard A. Clarke and Robert Knake. *Cyber War: The Next Threat to National Security and What to Do About It*. New York, NY: Ecco, 2010.

Gabriella Coleman. *Hacker, Hoaxer, Whistleblower, Spy: The Many Faces of Anonymous*. London: Verso, 2015.

Marc Goodman. *Future Crimes Inside the Digital Underground and the Battle for Our Connected World*. New York, NY: Anchor, 2016.

Heather Harrison Dinniss. *Cyber Warfare and the Laws of War*. Cambridge, London: Cambridge University Press, 2014.

Lech Janczewski and Andrew M. Colarik. *Cyber Warfare and Cyber Terrorism*. Hersey, PA: Idea Group Reference, 2008.

Fred M. Kaplan. *Dark Territory: The Secret History of Cyber War*. New York, NY: Simon & Schuster, 2016.

George Lucas. *Ethics and Cyber Warfare: The Quest for Responsible Security in the Age of Digital Warfare*. Oxford, London: Oxford University Press, 2016.

Paulo Shakarian, Jana Shakarian, and Andrew Ruef. *Introduction to Cyber-warfare a Multidisciplinary Approach*. Amsterdam, Netherlands: Elsevier/Syngress, 2013.

Peter W. Singer and Allan Friedman. *Cybersecurity and Cyberwar: What Everyone Needs to Know*. New York, NY: Oxford University Press, 2014.

Gabriel Weimann. *Terrorism in Cyberspace: The Next Generation*. New York, NY: Columbia University Press, 2015.

Steve Winterfeld and Jason Andress. *The Basics of Cyber Warfare Understanding the Fundamentals of Cyber Warfare in Theory and Practice*. Amsterdam, Netherlands: Elsevier, 2013.

Kim Zetter. *Countdown to Zero Day: Stuxnet and the Launch of the World's First Digital Weapon*. New York, NY: Crown, 2014.

Periodicals and Internet Sources

Ian Bremmer. "Cyber Crime Like the OPM Hack Is a Major Threat to the U.S." *Time*. Time, Inc., 19 June 2015.

"Cybercrime and Punishment." *Infosecurity*. Reed Exhibitions, Ltd., 02 Sept. 2014.

Matthew Dallek. "To Understand The Future Of Cyber Power, Look To The Past Of Air Power." *The World Post*. The Huff Post, 30 Mar. 2017.

Larry Greenemeier. "Here's What a Cyber Warfare Arsenal Might Look Like." *Scientific American*. Nature America, Inc, 6 May 2016.

Michael Holloway. "Stuxnet Worm Attack on Iranian Nuclear Facilities." *Stanford University*. 16 July 2016.

David Ignatius. "The Cold War Is Over. The Cyber War Has Begun." *Washington Post*. 15 Sept. 2016.

Adrienne LaFrance. "Cyberwar Is Officially Crossing Over Into the Real World." *The Atlantic*. The Atlantic Monthly Group, 16 May 2017.

Robert McMillan and Shane Harris. "In Modern Cyber War, the Spies Can Become Targets, Too." *Wall Street Journal.* Dow Jones & Company, 24 May 2017.

Evan Osnos. "How Not to Freak Out About Cyber War." *New Yorker.* Conde Nast, 15 Mar. 2017.

Jose Pagliery. "The Emergence of the 'cyber cold war.'" *CNNTech.* Cable News Network, 19 Jan. 2017.

Mattathias Schwartz. "Cyberwar for Sale." *New York Times.* The New York Times Company, 04 Jan. 2017.

Yaron Steinbuch. "Massive Cyberattack Spreads around the Globe." *New York Post.* NYP Holdings, Inc., 12 May 2017.

Simon Tisdall. "Cyber-warfare 'is Growing Threat.'" *The Guardian.* Guardian News and Media Limited, 03 Feb. 2010.

"War in the Fifth Domain." *The Economist.* The Economist Newspaper, 03 July 2010.

Mark Ward. "Smart Machines v Hackers: How Cyber Warfare Is Escalating." *BBC News.* BBC, 10 Mar. 2017.

George Will. "The Destructive Threat of Cyberwarfare." *National Review.* 13 Apr. 2016.

Fareed Zakaria. "Cyberwarfare Is the Real Menace to America." *Daily Herald.* Paddock Publications, Inc., 10 Mar. 2017.

Index